THE MAGIC OF LASTING LOVE

Other books by Joel D. Block, Ph.D.

Friendship: How to Give It, How to Get It
To Marry Again
The Other Man, The Other Woman: Understanding
and Coping with Extramarital Affairs

THE MAGIC OF LASTING LOVE

JOEL D. BLOCK, Ph.D.

CORNERSTONE LIBRARY
PUBLISHED BY SIMON & SCHUSTER, INC.
NEW YORK

Copyright © 1982 by Joel D. Block

All rights reserved
including the right of reproduction
in whole or in part in any form
Published by CORNERSTONE LIBRARY
A Division of Simon & Schuster, Inc.
Simon & Schuster Building
Rockefeller Center
1230 Avenue of the Americas
New York, New York 10020
Published by arrangement with Macmillan Publishing
Co., Inc.

CORNERSTONE LIBRARY and colphon are
registered trademarks of Simon & Schuster, Inc.

10 9 8 7 6 5 4 3 2 1

Manufactured in the United States of America

Library of Congress Cataloging in Publication Data

ISBN: 0-346-12589-8

Block, Joel D.
  The magic of lasting love.

  Reprint. Originally published: Lasting love. New
York: Macmillan, 1982.
  Bibliography: p.
  1. Love. 2. Marriage—Psychological aspects.
I. Title.
BF575.L8B557   1983   646.7′8   83-7860

To my mate, lover, and friend,

Gail

Contents

PART IV

PART V

PART VI

PART VII

PART VIII

Acknowledgments

I am indebted to the many individuals who have shared their relationship distress, fears, and hopes with me over the past decade. Their wisdom, failings, and rich experiences have stimulated me to put this volume together.

William Lederer and the late Don Jackson, in their ground-breaking book *The Mirages of Marriage*, first sparked my interest in family systems. Their contribution holds strong today, nearly fifteen years after my original introduction. Among the professionals who have influenced me in recent years are two whom I have never met: Dr. Richard Stuart and Dr. Robert L. Weiss. Dr. Stuart's masterful text *Helping Couples Change* provided the basis for several of the "relationship principles," and Dr. Weiss' prolific output through the Oregon University Marital Studies Program has had immense impact on my thinking and practice. Dr. Weiss' influence is also felt in *Marital Therapy*, a pioneering work by psychologists Neil Jacobson and Gayla Margolin. In turn, the social learning approach of Drs. Jacobson and Margolin has contributed to my work, particularly in the area of conflict resolution.

I am especially grateful to one of my former mentors, Dr. Albert Ellis. Dr. Ellis's critical mind and fine theoretical contributions continue with me although it has been several years since I enjoyed a two-year postdoctoral Fellowship under his tutelage.

Thanks are also due to Alice Castellucci, who offered encouragement and useful criticism, and who typed and retyped various drafts of the manuscript. Her sure hand helped to make the manuscript more readable. Thanks to Stacy Olivieri for typing the final draft. My wife, Gail, as ever, served as my on-site editor and inspiration. To say the very least, her presence makes the struggle so much more pleasant. My children, Abbey and Fred, through their delight in me, provide the joy so necessary for a book on relationships.

Author's Note

The identities of the people described herein were protected by altering names and various other external characteristics; the essential psychological and social dynamics involved have been preserved. Any resemblance to real persons is strictly intentional; any identification with particular persons is, I trust, impossible.

The terms "husband and wife," "him and her," "relationship and marriage," require clarification. Often the conventional "him" was used because it is awkward to say "him or her" each time I referred to an individual whose gender was inconsequential; so, too, the use of "wife," "husband," and "marriage" is not meant to exclude nonmarried readers, male or female. Indeed, it is my hope that the principles outlined in this book will prove helpful to any two people engaged in an ongoing love relationship.

PART I

Introduction

During the mid 1970s, I was engaged in an extensive research project involving over two thousand people. My goal was to examine the meaning and patterns of friendship attachments in our lives. In 1980 the end product of that effort was published in a book, *Friendship*. I found, through my five-year journey into the unexplored terrain of the friendship landscape, a diverse and sometimes surprising picture of relationships in America. By far, friendship was most common among women. Rich friendships were seldom to be found among men; and, sadly, friendships between the sexes—even when the couple were joined by marriage—was the exception. Scarcely more than one-third of the married respondents regarded their mates as friends! Those in living-together arrangements fared no better.

Some couples, battle-worn from the psychological war they waged, had withdrawn completely and left no room for intimacy in their lives. Whether they simply parted from a living-together agreement, pursued the formality of divorce in the case of marriage, or continued together unsatisfactorily, they were disillusioned. Others, discouraged but undaunted, still hungered for a closeness that eluded them. A minority achieved it. Under these circumstances, it is not difficult to imagine how a preoccupation with self-absorption evolved. We turned to self-love, separateness, independence, doing your own thing, with the hope of emotional salvation. For many, "Me" still reigns as the new god. We have gone from Barbra Streisand's "People Who Need People" to Paul Simon's "Fifty Ways to Leave Your Lover."

The new narcissism is evident in the proliferation of therapists who declare we should be our own best friends, devote ourselves to self-growth and self-actualization, and look out, above all, for "No. 1." As a result, our society, particularly in the last decade, has been off balance, with too much emphasis on self and not nearly enough appreciation for the equally necessary and different struggle for union.

As a psychologist and marital therapist, I am no more immune to relationship struggles than anyone else. After seventeen years of marriage, the rough periods have unsettled me as they may have you. Yet I take the firm position that it is a mistake to assume that individual growth can take precedence over relationships; the effort ceases to be growth because we cannot expand without involvement outside ourselves.

We can learn through relationships to look with the eyes of another person, to listen with another's ears and to feel with another's heart. We live in a social world, and the ability to develop an intimate relationship with at least one other person is vital to our well-being. Nothing teaches a person so much about other human beings as trying to live with another person. Nowhere can more be gained or lost, more lessons learned or energy squandered. In our search for the source of unhappy states, it is time that we got beyond the deep recesses of the unconscious and explored the nature of our relations with others.

Of the many relationships that can be examined equally well by the principles herein—parent-child, student-teacher, business partners, and the like—it is the long-term committed-bond between men and women that draws my interest in this volume. The book is designed to help such couples—regardless of their marital status—make their love last. Such books are far from rare, which may emphasize the extent to which couples need and seek this kind of assistance. I believe this book breaks new ground, however. The content is derived from the forefront of behavioral science and clinical experience; I have strived to go beyond vague advice, to prescribe definite procedures and principles that have been tried and found helpful in improving relationships.

In order to personalize the approach, a plethora of "corrective prescriptions" are presented along with each of the relationship principles. While the book's contents are intended to be covered in sequence, it is expected that the reader, in collaboration with his partner and the Relationship Inventory provided, will sample selectively. The contents are organized in a manner that allows a couple to focus on one segment of their relationship at a time and to develop their own pace of improvement. Whether a couple proceeds on their own or with the assistance of a professional therapist, it makes good sense to take small, manageable steps. An ailing or neglected relationship, in fact, may be compared to a physically out-of-shape person. Conditioning is best accomplished gradually and persistently; plunging into heavy training often leads to unnecessary injury and discouragement.

Although the directives in this book can bring about radical change—and, in that sense, they are revolutionary—what follows is neither a formula for instant improvement nor a game or gimmick. It is, rather, a program of hard work. It can be demanding and emotionally draining. It can lead to occasional failures as well as to success, to sadness as well as to exultation. I do not promise a relationship devoid of problems. Not even therapy can elevate a relationship to a state of constant euphoria. Such a condition does not exist in life—except, perhaps, in our fantasies.

Those who decide to strengthen their relationship should be prepared to deal with all of this, for there is no such thing as growth without pain. I urge you to make the effort. It is a wise investment; it is an opportunity to escape the chains of past disappointment and hurt by building constructively for now and the future.

INSIDE A FAILING RELATIONSHIP: MICHAEL AND LINDA

The scene is an exclusive seaside restaurant. A couple in their mid-forties are having dinner. Michael is deeply tanned, prosperous-looking. Linda, a former model, now a Ph.D. candidate in sociology, has bright green eyes and a lightly freckled face under a fluff of reddish brown hair. Michael and Linda Wilson have been married eighteen years. They are aware of each other, but only vaguely. This night, as on many others, their attention is directed elsewhere; presently their eyes and ears are trained on a younger couple seated nearby —a man and woman locked in each other's gaze, speaking softly, inaudibly, sometimes laughing together, other times looking very serious, playful, and earnest, all the while holding hands.

Michael and Linda, disconnected for many years, share a silent thought: Were we ever like that? If we were, what happened? When did the bottom fall out? The bottom, of course, did not suddenly fall out. Relationships do not abruptly collapse. Life is a process. People don't break; they slowly melt. The Wilsons, who once thought they had it made, failed or refused to recognize the signals, flashing over nearly two decades, that they hadn't.

Relationships crumble, finally, when each blames the other for failing to live up to the original visions that impelled the alignment: "I would have made something of myself had it not been for you!" or "I could have married someone who would have made me happy. Why did I choose you?" The "why" is probably unanswerable. Analysis brings, at best, conjectured responses: A man may want a hostess, a mother, an accessory, a centerfold, a sister, a slave, or a tyrant. A woman may crave a father, a son, a savior, or escape from home. Few of us marry out of mature love. We join together out of hope, and we hope that our fantasies will spring to life. We dream of love, but developing a loving relationship is another matter.

The Wilsons began with the dream of love—and not much more. Although Michael and Linda are both highly intelligent and well educated, they were naive and ill informed when it came to the skills and realities of maintaining a long-term relationship. Neither understood the need for being "relationship educated," since the state of "being in love" was supposed to automatically ensure a happy, vital union. As they grew through adulthood together, there were no mentors to tell them that marriage, involving two complex and ever-changing individuals with two equally complex and rapidly changing children, precludes continuous and perfect harmony, or that economic conditions, illness, in-laws, and aging would influence and stress their relationship.

Each confirmed for the other the mistaken notion that the first few months of intimate relating forms the period during which all problems "get ironed out." The implication is that people are static and that a relationship is also static. Of course, nothing could be further from the truth; couples who sit passively by, hoping that "every day things will get better and better," are inviting disaster. In fact, considering the expectations we hold for this fragile bond—heightened sexual passion, continuous love, emotional security, stimulating companionship, thorough compatibility—it is no wonder that some two-fifths of all divorce actions are initiated during the first two years of marriage.

The collision between expectation and reality was not immediate for the Wilsons. They were sheltered by intense infatuation during their courtship, and by the demands and pressures of family life in the beginning years of their marriage. Linda recalls:

"After the first year of marriage our son was born, I stopped modeling and settled into the life of the suburban domesticate—chief cook, bottle washer, chauffeur, and occasional tennis player. I was very involved in child raising, community affairs, and house ownership. Michael worked with tenacity and single-mindedness to put himself through college; he earned a degree in economics in four years while holding down a full-time job. Working by day in a brokerage firm, going to school at night and all summer, he lived on four hours of sleep for weeks at a time. After he got his bachelor's degree, he took further course work and earned his master's degree in business administration. By then he was very successful in the stock market. Unfortunately, though, we really didn't get to know each other; both of us were too consumed in our own worlds. I was absorbed at home with two pre-schoolers and was not particularly interested in Michael's business activities. He had a similar disinterest in, or perhaps even distaste for, my domestic posture."

During these early years, the Wilsons had a marriage of convenience. It was comfortable but only minimally companionable. Although they were pleasant with each other, their interests, goals, and life views were gradually diverging. Discussions exploring beliefs, inner feelings, likes and dislikes, and plans for the future became almost nonexistent. In striking contrast to the enthusiasm of courtship, conversation at times was painfully strained. Michael comments:

"Linda and I had at least two essentials that seem important for a good marriage: We respected each other, and we were attracted to each other sexually. That, according to many people (particularly our parents), should have been enough. But it wasn't; there was a large, hollow gulf in between our sexual contacts. There was only a minimum of talk; and what there was, more often than not, involved the business of marriage: 'Did you pick up milk?' 'Who's driving Kevin to soccer?' 'Did anyone call?' We didn't fight a lot or even disagree much. That wasn't the problem then. There was no fun in our relationship; none of that delightful intimacy and joyfulness that is associated with lovers."

Indeed, a large-scale research effort conducted through Cornell University revealed that the average parents of preschool children talk to each other only about half as much per day as they did during their first intimate years of marriage. This in itself is not necessarily corrosive; the dwindling quantity is minor compared to the painful change of quality. Researchers found conversation, once spiced with exchanges about books, ideas, and personal relationships, became almost entirely concerned with routine affairs—"What did you do today, dear?" . . . "Oh, nothing much . . . What did you do?" . . . "Was there anything in the mail?" . . . "The plumber came to fix the sink." In effect, husbands and wives were using the casual, more mundane words of dispassionate roommates rather than the warm and intimate words of lovers—not sometimes, but most of the time.

After the Wilsons coasted in their unsatisfactory but stable marriage for several years, financial setbacks produced the first real arena of open conflict for them. This was a stormy and bitter period; for them to acknowledge and openly deal with conflict was tantamount to admitting to failure. Rather than viewing disagreement as an inevitability, they viewed it as evidence that they were no longer in love. Against this backdrop, distress mounted. From Linda's experience:

"Michael had formed a partnership, and his company really began to move. He found out later on that his partner was a thief—he was stealing funds, gambling, using poor judgment —and, as a result, within two years we were broke. I found out that we had lost everything when Michael told me we had to sell the house. I was devastated. I was enraged that we were in this insecure position and that Michael hadn't informed me of what was going on. I reacted to his mismanagement by taking over and making unilateral financial decisions. Michael, feeling emasculated, used credit cards to make expensive purchases we couldn't pay for. It was as if he were saying, 'I'll show you I'm still boss around here.' My reaction was to attack him, to get back by 'forgetting' to make supper, embarrass him in front of his friends, put him down to the children. Anything to hurt him."

Other factors conspired to exacerbate this heightening war between Michael and Linda. Previously rewarding interactions had become stale and habitual, items of chronic complaint. For example, sex, after one thousand repetitions of ten minutes of foreplay followed by two minutes of thrusting in the missionary position, became less frequent and boring; their continued practice of the same limited shared activities—dining out, going to a movie—ceased to provide the enjoyment it had in the past. Communication became even more difficult; they often screamed at each other as a result of their growing frustration and alienation. Each responded to this unpleasantness with a burst of rage and further withdrawal. As displeasing behaviors proliferated, their overall satisfaction with the relationship plummeted. Both felt a loss of commitment, an inability to feel positive, and awaited the other's move to repair the marriage.

The experience of Michael and Linda Wilson highlights some of the ingredients of relationship distress. Many of us are at just such an impasse with the man or woman in our life, wherein a state of slow (and sometimes hastened) erosion is occurring. The process is characterized by the waiting game: "I'll respond to you only *after* you respond to me." Too often it is the divorce lawyer who gets the first response. While the development of an enduring relationship provides a degree of emotional fulfillment not afforded by other options in life, it is also more demanding than most of us realize. A long-term relationship must be thought of as alive; and, as with any living entity, it is constantly evolving, changing as it develops.

Yes, a love relationship can be especially joyous; but as

most couples are bound to find, achieving such a union is no small accomplishment. As a means of attaining fulfillment for two individuals, a long-term, committed relationship has limitations and imperfections. No other society, to my knowledge, expects so much from such a relationship—the source of all emotional satisfaction—as ours. Many couplings don't work —or they don't work for long. Stage, television, movies, and real life present us with frequent examples of relationship strife. It is likely that a goodly percentage collapses from mere overload.

A satisfying union, one that provides mutual pleasure, requires frequent repair and adjustment. Beyond the chemistry —the attraction between two people that defies analysis— what does it take to create a vital, lively, and productive relationship? Perhaps the ingredients for such a coupling cannot be fully accounted for, but neither are they completely elusive. The skill to resolve conflicts decisively must be developed; it is necessary to create new common interests and to keep growing as individuals, both to maximize involvement in shared pleasurable activities and to provide each other with new topics of conversation; rules are needed for the division of responsibility with provisos for overlap (recall the Wilsons' dilemma: "I was absorbed at home with two preschoolers and was not particularly interested in Michael's business activities. He had a similar disinterest in, or perhaps even distaste for, my domestic posture."); partners need to be able to express their feelings, both positive and negative, in an acceptable manner.

These, then, are the issues this volume will address: guidelines for increasing the "friendship feeling" most of us desire from our partner, development and reinforcement of communication and problem-solving skills, sexual enhancement, and suggestions for holding on to these gains. Despite the difficulties, it is quite possible to vitalize a relationship, to make love last. However, even with authoritative direction, considerable time and effort are usually required to achieve a desired result. Patience, the courage to change, and most of all the desire to grow are key ingredients. If this sounds like a tall order, consider that it probably requires as much work—energy, strength, and time—to support a bad alliance as to support a good one. Given a basic willingness, the "do-it-yourself" material that follows will not guarantee a perfect relationship but will provide excellent guidelines for a workable, reasonably satisfying one. Specifically, if the suggestions are studied and sincerely applied, several things are likely to occur:

1. Each partner will become more capable of contributing to the other's present and future goals.

2. Mutual support will be increased; both partners will enjoy a greater understanding of each other.

3. The degree of stimulation and companionship will be increased and expanded.

4. Disagreements and decisions will be collaboratively resolved.

5. Sensitive areas of the relationship will be explored more satisfactorily than previously.

6. The ability and willingness to adapt to changes that affect the relationship will be increased.

In the final analysis, each of us is the architect of our own relationships; perhaps the best assistance a book such as this can provide is a blueprint for the creation. Practically all of us hunger for a lasting, satisfying relationship. We have a great capacity—or, at least, a potential—for intimacy. Although it is not easy to develop—mutual growth is at times as painful and difficult as it is joyful and rewarding—it is worth the effort. In a period of rapid and sometimes chaotic social change, human relationships, especially long-term and intimate ones, offer something of value worth hanging on to. Even with its limitations, a committed relationship—whether or not it is sanctified by a marital decree—is, for many of us, one of the best and most enduring means of fulfillment.

FIRST PRINCIPLES: CHANGING

Since the beginning of time, human beings have expended immense energies in attempts to change members of their families—to make their sons, daughters, husbands, wives, and other relatives fit some idealized image. In our efforts to influence others, we have resorted to every imaginable device, from cruel and inhuman punishment to devious flattery. For the most part, these efforts have been unsuccessful; most of us resist—covertly or blatantly—the demand that we live up to others' visions of what we "should" be. The rebellion may take many forms—overeating, lack of cooperation, infidelity, or, in more extreme instances, suicide. In its active state, resistance to imposed change may result in chronic arguing, withdrawal, or complete estrangement. All of us strive to maintain our own identity as unique, independent persons. To frustrate this tendency is to ask for grief. So much for coercion.

At the same time that we resist imposed change, most of us would welcome direction for our *own* growth, both as individuals and as partners in a loving relationship. The questions people are asking reflect this concern: How do I deal with change? How can I contribute to a more satisfying relationship? What is needed in order for my relationship to blossom despite forces—pressures of making a living, differing preferences, precious little time, and the demands of children—that can impede that growth? In a world that is becoming more complex, we find ourselves confused about how to take the first steps toward relationship growth.

In an effort to diminish, if not dissolve, the confusion, three principles that defend individuality and challenge unwanted manipulation will be discussed. Contrary to those fruitless attempts to coerce our partners, the problem of how to control *ourselves* will be confronted. Taken together, the three principles that follow offer a new beginning, a method for fragmenting patterns of discord so that they may be replaced by behaviors that are positive and satisfying.

Perhaps the greatest obstacle to improving a relationship is the tendency to blame one's partner for the relationship discord. We seek simplistic answers even when there are none at hand. Right or wrong, who's at fault? Who's to blame? These become the predominant theme in a soured relationship. As any marital therapist can testify, both aggrieved spouses know who the culprit is: the other partner! All that remains, as far as each spouse is concerned, is enlightenment, that is, making that person see his or her fault, confess, and atone. To counter this combative tendency, consider the Principle of Individual Responsibility: *Each of us has the capacity to change. When we assign responsibility for our malaise to another person, we impede our change potential and become a victim.*

A couple has a fight. It begins because the wife feels irritated with her husband about something. They go to bed that evening without saying a word to each other. She is no longer angry and would like her husband to make contact with her —talk to her, reach out to her, caress her. He, not knowing that her mood has passed and fearing that she is still upset, does nothing of the sort, deciding to wait until she gives him some indication that she will respond to him more kindly. She is not willing to reach out and make contact herself, although she would like to do so. Lying there, she begins to blame him for not "making a move," for not doing something she herself is unwilling to do.

A wife feels ill at ease going to a restaurant, a theater, or any public place unaccompanied. She asks her husband to take her to a movie. He would rather watch a football game on television, so suggests she go alone and that afterward they meet for dinner. She responds with "Why are you so selfish?" and refuses to speak to him all evening.

A husband is a very poor manager of money. His debts pile up unpaid. His one major avenue to recovery is to file for a substantial federal income tax refund dating back several years. He procrastinates despite his wife's pleading. The bills continue to pile up, adding more pressure to the couple's tensions. Finally, the husband files for his refund and receives a prompt reply from the Internal Revenue Service stating that his request exceeded the cutoff date and was no longer valid. He immediately blames his wife, saying she should "have kept after him." When she grows angry and tells him that his failure to get things done is driving her to distraction, he continues to deny personal responsibility and escalates the blame to a new level. "If it was that important to you," he says, "why didn't you lock me out of the house or something until I filed the return?"

In the above examples, the blamer has the attitude, "I'm not responsible, you are." From this follows "If you are responsible for my (our) discomfort, distress, or unhappiness, only you can alter it." The following statements, based on those suggested by William Lederer and Don Jackson in their classic text *The Mirages of Marriage*, are characteristic of this attitude:

"If you treated me as though you really loved me, I could accomplish anything."

"If you would only accomplish something, I could really love you."

"If you would only make me feel welcome, I'd be home all the time and I'd be loving."

"If you stopped going golfing so often and stayed home more, I wouldn't act so nasty."

"If only you didn't drink so much, I wouldn't be so bitchy."

"If you weren't so bitchy, I wouldn't drink so much."

"If you encouraged me instead of condemning me, I would be a success."

"If you would only do things right, I would be so appreciative."

"If you were only more informed and well read, I would have more to say to you."

"If only you paid attention to me and showed me that my opinion counted, I would feel more confident in expressing it."

"If you didn't interrupt me whenever I started talking, I'd feel my remarks were more worthwhile and I'd be more sociable with your friends."

"If only you wouldn't embarrass me in front of my friends, I wouldn't be so hostile."

"If only you'd stop pampering the children, I would become more involved in parenting."

"If only you'd become more involved with the children, I wouldn't have to be both mother and father to them."

"If you'd hold my hand and pay attention to me at parties, I'm sure I'd never flirt again."

"If only you weren't such a flirt at parties, I wouldn't have to compete for your attention."

If it would help the relationship for the wife to be less flirtatious and the husband to be more attentive at parties, who is to take the initiative? And will the person making the first move be regarded by the spouse as having been wrong all along? When couples relate in such a blame-oriented way, they create a major obstacle to relating. Nothing is resolved if both husband and wife are constantly screaming or silently sulking about who is to blame. Resolution is unlikely unless one partner is willing to take on-the-spot initiative. He or she must drop the victim role.

Typically, in the blame-counterblame trap, as Lederer and

Jackson observed, both partners issue their complaints after the unwanted behavior has occurred but do nothing while it is taking place. A husband may accuse his wife of being inconsiderate because she repeatedly interrupts him. He will nag, complain, sulk, and admonish, but rarely will be take a firm stand while the behavior is actually happening. What if while being interrupted he stated "You're interrupting me, Barbara. Please let me finish what I'm saying"? If this didn't work, he might simply get up and leave the room, saying, "It seems, by your constant interruptions, that you are not interested in what I'm saying. When you feel more like listening, let me know." Although this behavior may seem harsh, it would probably work.

Jane harbors resentment toward Bill because he doesn't pay attention to her at social gatherings. Yet this behavior has continued on Bill's part for a long period of time, so it is likely that Jane has been blaming and antagonizing him rather than taking responsibility for getting what she wants: more attention. Perhaps she goes off in a corner at parties to sulk or becomes nasty and sarcastic about Bill's social adroitness. Later, when they are alone, she may withdraw or explode and tell Bill his behavior makes her furious. Her comments will then escalate their conflict into a fight or mutual withdrawal. If Jane would take responsibility for her shyness, envy of her husband's social popularity, or desire for more attention, instead of waiting for him to "save her," a major stumbling block to a functional relationship would be removed. This might involve inhibiting blaming statements, working to overcome her social shyness, and making a concerted effort to be part of her husband's conversations instead of withdrawing from them. Jane's initiative could break the cycle of mutual recrimination and restore the opportunity for productive relating.

Closely related to the proscription against blaming and withdrawing is the Principle of Reframing: *"To reframe" means to change one's viewpoint in relation to an event, to give a situation new meaning.* As the philosopher Epictetus expressed in the first century A.D., "People are disturbed not by things, but by the views which they take of them."

What governs behavior are our unique perceptions of ourselves and the world in which we live, the meanings we give to the events of our lives. This fact seems obvious enough, but in reality most of us do not appreciate the enormity of its application. Perhaps more than any other behavioral scientist, psychologist Albert Ellis has championed recognition of this principle. Ellis refers to it as the "ABC theory of personality and emotional disturbance," and stresses that it is not the activating events (A) that cause emotional consequences (C) but rather the individual's beliefs (B) about what occurred at point A.

According to Ellis, there are perhaps ten to fifteen mistaken beliefs that people hold to with costly results in terms of their individual and interpersonal effects. These include demands of perfection; insistence that life go smoothly; and the dictate that people act with absolute fairness and kindness. While it might be nice were we all very competent and the world didn't present us with petty and not-so-petty frustrations or that other people were always considerate, the devout insistence that therefore things *must* be that way leads to emotional upset and self-defeating behaviors.

Any number of examples may be cited to clarify the ABC philosophy, but let us take one typical occurrence as a case in point.

A man appears preoccupied much of the time and pays little attention to his partner (activating event). His partner decides that he has no regard for her feelings at all (belief system), so she becomes angry (consequence) and tears into him about his selfishness (another consequence). Now the woman blames her partner for *making* her angry. According to Ellis's approach, the woman's anger and outburst is under *her control, not her husband's.*

She could have viewed his behavior in several other ways;

for example, "He may be worried about something" or "He really gets involved in his work" or "He has difficulty managing his time" or "He simply requires less companionship." Even if the husband were acting selfishly, what guarantee is there that he must behave desirably all the time? Accepting her husband's low need for companionship (which is equivalent to reasonable tolerance, not preference) or viewing his behavior in less inflammatory terms would have enabled this woman to react in a more effective manner.

The point here is this: All behavior is open to many interpretations, and the particular interpretation chosen is crucial to the feelings and behavioral reactions that are generated. Discordant interaction arises when one mate views the other's behavior negatively (often in the worst possible manner) and *insists* that his or her perception is right and that the other partner change, all the while feeding into this downward spiral by reacting spitefully and demandingly. Then the other mate, by dwelling on the negative reaction ("That S.O.B. isn't going to get away with this"), escalates his or her behavior and an outburst of temper on the part of both spouses ensues. According to the principle of reframing, instead of being carried along feeling powerless and without control, we must accept responsibility for our own fate. It is *our* choice to make or to refuse to make ourselves seriously distressed. The effort to train ourselves to reframe—"How can I view this situation in the most productive (and realistic) manner possible?"—is likely to be rewarded by increased harmony and avoidance of unnecessary stress.

Since our individual interpretations of behavior are largely the product of experience, there is no more fruitful way of affecting or changing those interpretations than through new kinds of experience. It is rare that we are successful in changing perceptions either in ourselves or in others simply by "willing," unless this process is accompanied by some kind of experience as well.

Such change may be accomplished through open discussions with others in which beliefs can be explored and subjected to the impact of other personalities. Sometimes old perceptions can be examined in a more solitary fashion, as when we set ourselves the task of "thinking through" an idea. Occasionally, creative activities like painting or music or writing aid the process. Perhaps the most important way in which individuals can arrive at a new understanding of behavior is through the deliberate breaking out from accustomed patterns, in other words, changing one's own behavior.

In a sense, change requires a kind of flirting with inadequacy, the courage to fumble, a willingness to open ourselves to a degree of pain in the present in the hope that greater satisfaction will be derived in the long run. Something must be ventured if there is to be any gain. This, of course, is not easy and brings us to what Dr. Richard Stuart in *Helping Couples Change* calls the Fear-of-Change Principle: *Although we may want to change our responses and behaviors, we do not necessarily welcome the change. In most areas of our lives, we put a premium on security and resist change even if the novel behavior is toward the relief of pain and the promise of pleasure.*

Given that an individual has at least the requisite skills for creating desired relationship changes, there are a number of obstacles to be overcome. Frequently, both spouses feel they have been victimized in the relationship, giving more than they have received. Both partners, as we have seen, typically decide to withhold positive changes on the basis of pride; they feel that "giving in" implies they have been wrong all along. In essence, they adopt a "change-second" rather than a "change-first" attitude, which results in a hopeless deadlock.

Just as false pride makes progress more difficult, inertia also comes into play. This is the tendency for an established pattern to remain unaltered. In order for us to move forward, an extra push is needed. Once the initial energy is exerted and change is well under way, less effort will be required. But it is often

onerous to exert this extra energy, and balking as well as rebellion is to be expected.

It is fear, though, that exerts the most powerful influence in
the change process. Fear is the feeling that engulfs us when we
seriously consider altering a pattern that is well established,
even if it is dysfunctional.

Edward Henley, a forty-five-year-old journalist, knows this
feeling well. Depressed for many months, out of desperation
he followed his physician's advice and consulted a psychologist. Now, three months after a year-long therapy experience,
he discusses his struggle to confront his fear:

"At first, the idea of psychological help seemed strange to
me. I wondered, 'How can this help me—just talking about
things that aren't even clear to me?' But I found that talking,
having to put my vague thoughts into words, forced me to
think of things I hadn't considered in many years; it had the
effect of making me dig deep inside myself and bring up things
I hardly knew were troubling me. As we continued to meet, I
spoke more easily of my relationship with my wife, Mary. In
one conversation, I felt as if I had come to the edge of an
awful canyon; I referred to it later as a pit I had dug for
myself. I became aware that all these years were spent avoiding involvement with Mary. I really had no intimacy; after
seventeen years of marriage, I wasn't close to her or to anyone
else. If Mary was getting too close, I busied myself with work,
limiting the amount of time I spent with her; even if I revealed
a personal feeling, I did so in a controlled manner, making
sure not to be *too* revealing. Basically, I had this feeling that if
Mary, or anyone else for that matter, really got to know me, I
would be a total disappointment. I guess I don't have much
value in myself as a person.

"At one point in our conversation, I remarked that I
haven't let myself really be loved by anyone. The statement
was true and it was agonizing, but there was still a buffer
between the words and my experience. It wasn't quite real, it

didn't penetrate my armor. The therapist asked me to repeat my statement slowly and as I did so to focus on my feelings. I did it once and I started to feel weak; I felt wobbly even though I was seated. He asked me to do it again, and I tried but I could barely speak. I felt more deeply disturbed than I can describe; I had reached a point far away from anything I had ever known. Despair, fear, and grief, all greater than I had felt before, were evoked by the thought of changing, increasing my vulnerability to hurt. Suddenly, I was engulfed in emotion beyond anything I had ever experienced.

"As soon as the session ended, I went home and forced myself to sleep. I was scared and unhappy when I woke up. I couldn't rid myself of the thought that I had withdrawn from significant human contacts; I was not even intimate with myself. I would not allow myself to experience my feelings about myself, and I managed to avoid the intensity of the previous conversation. I was angry and confused, afraid of what I felt and even more frightened of what I needed to do in order to change. I felt lost, and for the first time since childhood I felt real panic. I skipped several appointments in an effort to run away from what I was feeling, but I found those feelings impossible to deny. The therapist encouraged me gently but persistently to risk being open, to let things happen to my feelings, and to expose them. Gradually, I was even able to reveal more of my 'true self' to Mary."

Fear can be obvious and overpowering, as in the case of Mr. Henley. In other instances, fear makes its appearance in a more subtle or deceptive manner: excuses, bravado, lethargy, helplessness, rebellion, resentfulness, and the like. Whatever the form, fear is practically always a part of the change process, and its presence demands respect—pushing too hard is likely to be met with resistance. Lack of challenge, on the other hand, will encourage the status quo.

The transformation required in order for a relationship to become rewarding is, of course, neither simple nor instant. There is not one dramatic issue to be repaired but a series of little separations which, over time, eat away at the emotional connection. To avoid the pitfalls inherent in the change process, a number of suggestions are offered.

1. *Be gradual.* A great many attempts at change fail because they are too sweeping in nature. The attempt to change a relationship too quickly or too greatly in too short a period of time is responsible for a good deal of the disillusionment and despair many people feel. For example, when a woman is dissatisfied with her partner's participation in household chores, she may request broad changes in his behavior, in which case he is quite likely to resist, since the request for change will be perceived as overwhelming. However, if the requests are gradual and successively approximate the desired level of participation, the process of change is likely to proceed more smoothly.

2. *Expect resistance.* Compounding the difficulty we all have with the change process is the fact that change in relationships often involves the risk of moving closer to another person. While we want the rewards of closeness, many of us fear the increased vulnerability and possibility of hurt that accompany intimacy.

3. *Be persistent.* Both parties can be expected to test the sincerity of each other's change efforts. Testing may take the form of provocation, questioning of motivation ("You're doing this only because you're afraid I'll leave you") in an attempt to discount the change effort, expressing feelings of hopelessness ("These changes are just too artificial and trivial") and/or a return to earlier behaviors. By viewing testing as a natural part of the change process and continuing with the novel behavior pattern despite temporary discouragement, a new precedent is set.

4. *Be positive.* It is much easier to increase positive behavior than it is to directly eliminate negative behavior. For example, rather than emphasizing a suppression of excessive criticism, a spouse is likelier to be effective if he or she concentrated on a response incompatible to criticism—an increase in positive, appreciative comments. Behavioral

science research suggests that undesirable behaviors are more effectively controlled when confronted in this positively oriented manner.

5. *Be behavioral*. Although feelings and beliefs are critically important in a relationship, neither carries the impact reserved for action. Telling a partner of your love does not have the immediacy and potency of a demonstration. Relationship change, therefore, is founded on paying close attention to what you do—"Am I behaving in a manner that promotes relationship satisfaction?"—rather than simply what you profess.

Finally, it might be noted that when both partners are trying—where there is respect for the identity, equality, and integrity of the other—obstacles to change can be successfully worked out. When we are willing to renounce the support of the familiar, take initiative, and view our partner's behavior compassionately, the possibilities are very promising indeed.

RELATIONSHIP-ENHANCEMENT INVENTORY

Before beginning with the Relationship-Enhancement Principles, a brief inventory to establish how each partner assesses and perceives the relationship will be given. The inventory is divided into three sections:

1. *Support*. This is concerned with behaviors that set the tone of the relationship.
2. *Communication*. This is concerned with the manner in which messages are conveyed.
3. *Conflict resolution*. This is concerned with the manner in which disagreements are handled.

The function of the inventory is to identify areas where improvement is needed. It is not intended to instigate fault-finding. Each item is to be answered independently of the others, and each partner is to take the inventory separately. Base your responses on your feelings over the past two weeks; that is, do not be biased by a particular incident, positive or negative. Instead, consider an overall assessment over a prolonged period.

Support

1. My partner treats me as an equal; he/she promotes the idea that I am worthy of respect.

1	2	3	4
rarely true	slightly or occasionally true	sometimes or moderately true	almost always true

2. My partner shows appreciation or acknowledges when I do or say something nice.

1	2	3	4
rarely true	slightly or occasionally true	sometimes or moderately true	almost always true

3. I enjoy spending time with my partner.

1	2	3	4
rarely true	slightly or occasionally true	sometimes or moderately true	almost always true

4. I am willing, without feeling resentful, to pitch in if my partner needs help to carry out his/her responsibilities.

1	2	3	4
rarely true	slightly or occasionally true	sometimes or moderately true	almost always true

5. My partner and I do a great deal to express our caring for each other.

1	2	3	4
rarely true	slightly or occasionally true	sometimes or moderately true	almost always true

6. I make every effort to view my partner's actions in a positive manner.

1	2	3	4
rarely true	slightly or occasionally true	sometimes or moderately true	almost always true

7. I feel that the effort required to make the relationship work is equitably distributed.

1	2	3	4
rarely true	slightly or occasionally true	sometimes or moderately true	almost always true

Communication

1. I feel understood by my partner when we discuss personal relationship issues.

1	2	3	4
rarely true	slightly or occasionally true	sometimes or moderately true	almost always true

2. My partner is flexible; he/she is open to new ideas rather than the exclusive pursuit of his/her own point of view.

1	2	3	4
rarely true	slightly or occasionally true	sometimes or moderately true	almost always true

3. My partner knows when to listen and when to talk during our discussions.

1	2	3	4
rarely true	slightly or occasionally true	sometimes or moderately true	almost always true

4. I feel that my partner is interested in what I have to say.

1	2	3	4
rarely true	slightly or occasionally true	sometimes or moderately true	almost always true

5. My partner is open; he/she will reveal personal issues and feelings when the disclosures are likely to advance our discussion.

1	2	3	4
rarely true	slightly or occasionally true	sometimes or moderately true	almost always true

6. My partner speaks in a manner that is direct and to the point.

1	2	3	4
rarely true	slightly or occasionally true	sometimes or moderately true	almost always true

7. I can count on my partner's statements as being sincere.

1	2	3	4
rarely true	slightly or occasionally true	sometimes or moderately true	almost always true

Conflict Resolution

1. Discussing disagreements with my partner is productive; irrelevant issues and fault finding do not characterize the conversation.

1	2	3	4
rarely true	slightly or occasionally true	sometimes or moderately true	almost always true

2. I feel confident that discussions of conflict will not get out of control.

1	2	3	4
rarely true	slightly or occasionally true	sometimes or moderately true	almost always true

3. The agreements I make with my partner provide clarity as to who was to do what and when.

1	2	3	4
rarely true	slightly or occasionally true	sometimes or moderately true	almost always true

4. I trust my partner to keep his/her end of an agreement.

1	2	3	4
rarely true	slightly or occasionally true	sometimes or moderately true	almost always true

5. In general, discussing a disagreement leads to my feeling more hopeful and to identifiable changes in the relationship.

1	2	3	4
rarely true	slightly or occasionally true	sometimes or moderately true	almost always true

6. I feel I can strongly express my anger when I am highly disturbed.

1	2	3	4
rarely true	slightly or occasionally true	sometimes or moderately true	almost always true

7. Following a fight, we make up promptly and sincerely rather than carry a prolonged grudge.

1	2	3	4
rarely true	slightly or occasionally true	sometimes or moderately true	almost always true

Interpretation

If the total score for either partner on any section is twenty-one or less, it is an indication that improvement is necessary. However, low scores should be viewed *only* as a signal that improvement is desirable, not as proof that the relationship is incurably dysfunctional. The inventory is not a tested scientific instrument but merely a general guide for determining the need for improvement in each of the relationship-enhancement areas. In this regard, another assessment should be taken two weeks after completion of each group of principles so that a growth comparison can be obtained. Little or no positive change in scores should prompt a discussion of specific inventory items that indicate weak areas and are to be targeted for further improvement.

PART II

Increasing Mutual Support: The Power of Positive Expectations

There is a time-worn tale that in its simplicity has profound implications for interpersonal relationships. A city slicker driving down a country road one evening gets a flat tire. Much to his consternation, stranded on this lonely road, he discovers that he doesn't have a jack, an absolute necessity if he is to change tires and be on his way. Just as he is mentally preparing to sleep in the car and seek help in the morning, he recalls passing a farm a few miles back. "Why not give that a try?" he asks himself. "The weather is mild and I could make it in half an hour." With that, he locks the car and begins to hike.

Once under way, the city slicker starts thinking, "It's late at night, I'll probably wake the farmer, he'll be angry . . . Farmers don't like city folks, he'll be nasty . . . He probably won't trust me to bring back his jack anyway . . . I can just see this guy sneering at me, saying to himself, 'That dumb city slicker doesn't even know enough to keep a jack in his car!' " With that final thought, he arrives at the farmer's house, calls out, and the farmer opens his window. Before the farmer can utter a word, the city slicker shouts, "You can take your stinkin' jack and shove it!" That night the city slicker sleeps in his car.

Humans are continually rehearsing their reactions to anticipated future events. How we think about what awaits us, particularly in the near future, strongly influences our lives. Hope spurs us on; hopelessness, the inability to foresee satisfaction in the future, creates despair. Many of us are, in fact, despondent; we view our relationships as floundering and act accordingly, that is to say, with weakened commitment. We put little in because we expect little in return. And this is just what we get: a meager return. As with the city slicker, we expect negativism, communicate our anticipation, and get to "sleep in the car."

In sharp contrast, the hopeful person, expecting that an event will turn out well, signals his enthusiasm through facial expressions, stature, and confident attitude. Those who are involved with this person are encouraged by his display of self-assurance, are drawn in by his enthusiasm, and are likely to respond in kind. The law of expectations is simple: The way an event is viewed (how you expect it to turn out) will affect your behavior and, in turn, alter the actual outcome.

In one study of influence of expectations reported by Julius and Barbara Fast in *Talking Between the Lines*, a teacher was told that certain students in her new class were intellectually "gifted" and others were intellectually "dull." The teacher was advised that she could expect above-average performance by the "gifted" children; in contrast, it was suggested that below-average performance could be expected of the "dull" children. By the end of the school term, the labels "gifted" and "dull" had been affirmed, above-average and below-average performances being the respective outcome.

On the surface, the results of this study seem unexceptional. In fact, the outcome was quite remarkable, considering that all the students in the class were actually of average intelligence—none were "gifted" or "dull." The teacher had been intentionally misinformed about their learning potential to dramatize the self-fulfilling implications of expectations. When children honestly believe they can perform well or, conversely, that they are incompetent, they live up to those expectations.

The expectation study raised another question. In what way did the teacher communicate to some students that they were special and capable of superior work, and to others that they were slow and incapable of performing otherwise? Further investigation revealed the influencing factors to be the type of work the teacher presented each group, the way she presented it, and, most importantly, her attitude toward the two groups of students.

When she spoke to the "gifted" youngsters, there was an element of enthusiasm and interest in her voice that communicated "You're bright children, you can master this material." There was a reassurance in her tone that gently encouraged them to do their very best. When a "gifted" student's work did not measure up to expectation, the teacher was supportive, patient, and encouraging. The deviation was treated as a temporary lapse, a bad day. In contrast, the apprehensive tone of voice and lack of enthusiasm directed toward the "dull" students carried the message "This work is very difficult, you will have trouble with it." Poor work was responded to with annoyance and impatience. Sarcasm and put-downs were not uncommon. The "dull" students responded to this discouragement by behaving poorly, not listening to instructions, and not doing homework assignments—all factors resulting in impaired learning.

In another investigation, the experimenter wanted to examine the effects of expectations of interpersonal "warmth" and "coldness": How does the expectation that a person will be warm or cold influence actual impressions of that person? How do these expectations influence behavior toward this person? The subjects were sixty-five college students in three college classes. A person unknown to the students was introduced to each class as a temporary replacement for their regular instructor. Half of the members of each class were given biographical information about the substitute instructor, which included the statement that he was "rather cold." The remaining subjects were independently given identical information, except that it included the statement that the instructor was "very warm."

The instructor led each class in a twenty-minute discussion, a record being kept of each student's participation. Afterward, first-impression ratings of the instructor were obtained from all students. Comparison of the "warm" and "cold" expectation groups revealed impressions that strongly coincided with expectations: Those who anticipated a warm instructor described him as more considerate of others, less formal, more social, and more humorous than those who anticipated a cold instructor. "Warm" expecters also participated in the class discussion significantly more than the students given the "cold" expectation.

The main theme of these two studies (and of others covering such diverse topics as stuttering, psychological testing, and physical disability) is that expectations are major determinants of human behavior; expectations are both interpersonally communicated and influential of others' behavior. With this material as background, it becomes apparent that negative expectations ("He doesn't care about me and he never will") can become self-fulfilling prophecies. Discouraging and negative thoughts are communicated through grimaces, muscle tensing, chilling silences, tones of voice, or the more obvious periods of thoughtlessness ("Why should I, he doesn't . . ."). Whether or not these behaviors are intentional, reactions to them are usually negative and inflammatory. Quarreling often occurs, and the negative cycle is reinforced.

If negative expectations are so destructive, it is reasonable to suggest changing them, creating positive expectations. If only it were as simple as that. In many relationships, the negative cycle is well established and will not yield to mere suggestion; simply thinking about the relationship differently, although important, is not sufficient. Consistent and persistent *behavior* change is required. At this point a dilemma emerges:

If I think and feel negatively, how am I to behave lovingly? It is here that a very powerful strategy, the As-If Principle, described by the German philosopher Hans Vaihinger in 1877, comes into play.

The As-If-Principle is based on the notion that changing our beliefs about a person (including ourselves) is most effectively accomplished by acting *as if* the change had already been achieved. Noted psychologist George Kelly, among others, reported great success with this approach. Dr. Kelly encouraged his clients to act as if they did not have the problem that distressed them. The shy college student, for example, was instructed to act as if he were self-assured when he approached girls on campus, and the critical husband was asked to act toward his wife as if her behavior were acceptable.

Assuming that the skills are available (e.g., knowing how to act in a self-assured way) and the emotion (e.g., fear, anger, and the like) is not unusually intense, acting *as if* creates an opportunity to go beyond the past, to dispel old prejudices through reality testing. Even a bumbling effort, if viewed liberally, as a start, as a move in the right direction, initiates a new vision, provides a glimmer of what could be. This same principle is fundamental to all relationship restorative efforts. Commonly, for example, distressed partners complain of having lost their feelings of love. Not feeling loving, they do not act loving. And herein lies the stalemate: Feelings of love will not magically appear; they can only be renewed through loving interaction with a partner. Therefore, the key to revitalizing the relationship is to act *as if* you feel loving, for only then do you increase the probability of stimulating your love feelings as well as your partner's reciprocity. *Love is an effect of loving behavior*.

In brief, the sequence is to do something to feel something rather than to wait to feel something in order to do something. Every time you do something, the feelings and ideas consistent with that behavior are reinforced. It's as though the act recharges the feelings and beliefs that coincide with it. If you dislike someone, disparaging him and trying to hurt him will increase your feelings of dislike. If you want to increase your acceptance of another person, offer criticism very sparingly and compassionately, act in a manner that conveys approval. Again, if you want to increase love feelings, observe your behaviors for their consistency with that desire.

Of course, it is not likely that you can make yourself feel strongly positive toward someone you abhor simply by acting as if you love him. But a weakened love can be intensified by acting on it. Carl calls his wife at work and tells her, "I was just thinking of you and I wanted to say hello. Have you got time to talk?" That is an act of caring, the kind of small behavior that builds goodwill.

Consider it this way: Each time a relationship-promoting behavior is demonstrated, it is as if a deposit is made in a relationship account. Building up the account creates hopefulness, a positive expectation of the future. And, in fact, deposits do eventually yield interest. A high frequency of pleasing behavior creates the attitude "He (she) thinks well of me and tries to please me; I will do the same." What's more, an account with high-deposit activity can withstand occasional withdrawals in the form of displeasing behaviors. Deposits in the form of pleasing behaviors act as buffers against the sting of displeasing behaviors. Withdrawals are inevitable, but it is only in a depleted or overdrawn account, where pleasing behaviors are too few and hopefulness has been replaced by despair, that bankruptcy is likely to occur.

The principles that follow provide an opportunity for you to build up your relationship account and thereby create positive expectations, which in turn will yield positive responses. Taken together, these principles comprise the major elements of a supportive union: caring, trust, acceptance, physical stimulation, and autonomy. Indeed, a relationship is likely to succeed in proportion to the degree to which these ingredients are present.

THE PRINCIPLE OF EXPRESSED CARING

The Principle of Expressed Caring: A healthy relationship requires *active* concern on the part of each individual for the satisfaction and growth of the other.

An active caring or concern for the satisfaction and growth of another individual means that the concerned person *acts*, he engages in behavior aimed at providing the conditions of satisfaction and growth of the other. Those behaviors viewed as caring expressions may, of course, vary from person to person. One woman, a forty-four-year-old artist, married twenty years, expresses her views in this way:

"Caring doesn't mean rushing into action at every crisis and 'making it all better.' When a child falls and hurts herself, the mother who 'cares' too much glosses over the pain by mouthing words that are empty and unrealistic: 'There now, don't cry, that doesn't hurt.' What the child wants, though, is for her mother to understand how she really feels: 'There now, of course it hurts, no wonder you are crying. Soon it will mend and you will feel better.'

"For me, caring in an adult relationship is the same thing. If the quality of my work is disappointing, for example, I don't want someone to simply rationalize for me or entertain me into a frozen smile; someone who cares doesn't deny my feelings. I want, instead, someone who will listen carefully and try to understand. My husband doesn't do that; he is so caught up in his business that he simply dismisses my concerns out of hand: 'Oh, don't worry, things will work out.' I feel as if I hardly exist in his life. I've adjusted to that, but it saddens me and limits the relationship. More of my emotional investment is directed toward my women friends; they lend a sympathetic ear. It is with them that I really feel nurtured."

Caring, a feeling of mutual concern, is a much sought-after goal of individuals in a relationship. In a sense, the actively caring person can be thought of as a "supply source" of satisfactions; most of us are drawn to "suppliers," people who act positively toward us. It is in this atmosphere that we feel valued. Indeed, demonstrated caring is a very powerful relationship asset. Research evidence and clinical experience suggest that people tend to be more strongly attracted to others who behave toward them in a caring manner. *In fact, positive actions are likely to promote positive reactions, first in the attitudes of others, then in their behavior.* When an intimate demonstrates caring, we feel liked and in turn deepen our liking for this person. Thus, we acquire a vested interest in the satisfaction of an intimate, and by so doing we increase the chances for our own satisfaction. It's simple: a satisfied partner is better able and more willing to provide for our satisfactions than a dissatisfied partner. Marion, a woman married fifteen years to a man who travels extensively, describes her experience:

"When we were first married, I accompanied Sid on his trips to the Middle East, three or four times. The trips certainly were not fun; they were exhausting and often boring. Most of the time I spent alone in a hotel room while Sid tended to business. So I stopped going, and our contact was minimal and strained for long periods of time. Occasionally, we would write brief notes or phone, but only occasionally. I felt like a fixture in Sid's life and greeted him with a growl when he finally arrived home. Those were difficult days. When we were both just a slight push from the divorce lawyer's office, we sat down and had a very serious, thoughtful conversation. It wasn't feasible for Sid to change jobs, nor was it any longer very practical for me to accompany him—what would I do with two children? We talked about other ways to bridge the gap, to keep our feelings for each other alive.

"Now when Sid's away, he is more thoughtful of me. He phones several times a week. We both write long letters that are intimate and detailed. Those letters, sent special-class mail, reinforce our feelings for each other. Of course, I get lonely while Sid's away. But I plan ahead. I purchase theater and concert tickets, I let our friends know I'm available for dinner invitations. I do these things because it is better than stewing. I feel better about myself, I no longer feel neglected or sorry for myself; and, consequently, my attitude toward Sid is more positive when he returns. What's more, I spend a lot of time thinking about the relationship, our life together, planning shared time when he gets home. Sid does the same. When he comes home, we have all that to explore together."

Despite the span of thousands of miles and long periods apart, Marion and Sid were able to maintain their basis for intimacy. By demonstrating their caring for each other, they stayed involved, even under difficult circumstances. Unfortunately, despite the advantages of mutual and active caring, the experience proves elusive to many. Some couples are so preoccupied with notions of romantic love that opportunities for small but important caring gestures are overlooked. Even though a base hit would have been possible, these couples value only a home run and usually strike out. Others mistakenly believe that a post-honeymoon relationship moves along on its own energy and consequently do not bother to fuel it.

It is not uncommon for some couples to be so conflict-imbedded that it never occurs to them to begin their repair process with small, manageable, positive actions. *The attempt to resolve emotion-laden conflicts without a foundation of goodwill provided through the exchange of caring gestures is doomed.* It is analogous to the man or woman entering the professional athletes arena without prior conditioning. The effort is likely to be undermined. Typically, inflammatory and negative demands are exchanged, accusations are made, and both parties retreat to hurt silence until the next round begins.

Still other couples attempt to demonstrate their concern for each other but do so in a manner that is inappropriate. "I don't think my husband loves me anymore . . . He certainly doesn't show it if he does," Susan comments about her husband, Gary. She and Gary have been married ten years, and both feel increasingly neglected by the other. Gary expresses his caring in practical, "sensible" ways: Instead of bringing flowers, which soon wilt, he brings home new kitchen gadgets; rather than phoning from the office, he works straight through and often quite late, hoping to earn a promotion. To Gary these are caring expressions.

Of course, to Susan, who doesn't enjoy time in the kitchen and is opposed to making more money at the expense of family life, his efforts go unappreciated. Susan is more sentimental, less practical. She will buy Gary a pair of furry slippers because they look so inviting, so warm, and cannot understand Gary's annoyance with these gifts. "It's a waste," he complains. "My feet sweat in these things. Besides, I don't like slippers."

This may be one situation where the Golden Rule—"Do unto others as you would have others do unto you"—is not the right approach. Spouse A believes that he is behaving in a loving, benevolent manner toward Spouse B. In reality, A is behaving in an insensitive, even selfish, manner (*i.e.*, "If it pleases me, it should please you"). If B describes A's behavior as neglectful rather than caring, A is hurt and replies, "I was only trying to be loving."

George is an excellent cook. He does the shopping and prepares elaborate and rich meals regularly, which he regards as his way of expressing his love for Diane. Diane, however, is getting fatter by the month, her blood pressure is skyrocketing, and she is unhappy with herself. Diane tries to diet, but George makes it more difficult when he puts a hurt look on his face and explains how he spent the entire morning preparing that chocolate mousse she is refusing.

Is George's behavior simply misguided benevolence? Actually, George seems to be nurturing his own ego, upstaging

Diane with his fancy preparations, encouraging her to feel less attractive; his "caring" behavior is more likely a form of one-upmanship, selfishness, and lack of consideration, behavior all humans are capable of at times. The point is that considering this behavior to be loving is an expression of self-deception.

There are many other examples of behavior that appears to be caring but is really selfish, or what authors Lederer and Jackson term "pseudobenevolent." Consider, for instance, the spouse who is greeted effusively at the door upon his return home from work. His partner insists on fussing over him and relaxing him with a drink (he abhors the taste of alcohol) despite his insistence that he relaxes best by having a few moments of solitude. Or the husband who picks out the expensive gift—a new car, for instance—without first consulting with his wife. Often, the surprised recipient of such a purchase would have wanted to at least be given the option of choosing the model and accessories *she* wanted. Then there's the protective partner who irritates under the guise of caring by constantly asking, "Are you all right?" "Is everything OK?" Brief separations are infused with telephone calls, telegraphs, reminders to take this or that, all of which drives the recipient to distraction.

Corrective Prescription

Obviously, the generalized recommendation to be caring is too vague. If acts of "loving self-deception" are to be avoided, caring expressions must be developed in consideration of your partner's preferences. In that regard, a number of behavioral scientists, including Professor Richard Stuart of the University of Utah School of Medicine and William Lederer in his recent book *Marital Choices*, suggest an individually tailored program of caring exchanges, such as the one below, to be carried out over a two-week period.

In the "caring-behavior" exercise, each partner is to ask the other: What would you like me to do as a means of giving you support and showing my concern for you? Answers to this question are assembled in a combined list, which will be conspicuously posted. After questioning your spouse about *behaviors* (not feelings or attitude) he or she considers caring expressions, combine the list into one large chart. There are four criteria that a caring request must meet before qualifying for listing:

1. *The request must be specific and positive.* "Make good eye contact when we speak" is positive; "stop looking at the floor when we speak" is negative. "Offer suggestions about my work problems" is specific; "show me more consideration" is vague.

2. *The request must not be the focus of a recent conflict.* If frequency of sex is a burning issue, for instance, delay this agenda for the conflict-resolution procedures that come later.

3. *The behaviors must be of a type that can be performed at least once daily.* "Remembering special occasions" doesn't qualify; "kissing goodnight" does.

4. *The behaviors must be small, minor acts, those that can be easily performed.* Do not include something that requires your partner to have a personality overhaul in order to accomplish it. If your partner is generally talkative, for instance, don't request long periods of silence. Pages 46 and 47 show one couple's chart.

Notice that the chart on pages 46 and 47 contains numerous items. Experience suggests that at least eighteen entries should be listed in order to allow enough variation for each partner to sample a *minimum of four items daily*. If your chart comes up short, it may be helpful to recall some of the pleasing behaviors exchanged during the beginning phase of your relationship, those you practiced during happy times, and add them to the chart. If some of the listed behaviors appear unimportant or even trivial, do not be discouraged. These small gestures are designed to set the tone of a relationship and to pave the way for tackling thornier issues at a later date.

You will also notice that the manner in which the sample list is set up allows for record keeping. In addition to performing the requested behaviors, it is important to have accurate information about how many desirable behaviors have been generated within the relationship during the course of the two-week period. This written record helps each partner identify behaviors he or she may have overlooked; and, by each partner recording the other's actions, it provides an acknowledgment and encouragement of positive behavior. The record keeping is accomplished by the receiving spouse recording the date of the caring gesture in the giver's column next to the behavior description. As the dates are filled in, the chart serves as a visual reminder of the possibility of relationship improvement.

Important supplements to the caring-behavior program follow:

1. If you have children, you may want to include them in the program toward the end of the first week. Explain your attempt to show more concern for each other and patiently expand the chart to accommodate their participation. The caring-behavior chart is subject to review and revision at any time. Eliminate behaviors as they become outdated; add others as they are requested.

2. Each participant is to continue the caring expressions irrespective of whether or not the other participants are continuing to make similar gestures. It is not uncommon for one partner to test the other's commitment by unilaterally withdrawing. Gently put aside the excuses offered—"It's silly and artificial," "I don't have time," "This won't help"—and encourage commitment to the program.

3. At the end of each day, each participant is to leave a brief note for the other participants acknowledging at least one caring gesture.

Although the caring-behavior program may seem cumbersome, it actually proceeds quite smoothly and easily after a

A SAMPLE TWO-WEEK CARING-BEHAVIOR RECORD

(Dates of each occurrence of each behavior are to be recorded in spaces provided.)

	Husband						Wife				
	7/3	7/4	7/6	7/7	7/8	7/9	Offer a cheerful greeting when either of us arrives home.	7/3	7/4	7/5	7/8	7/11 7/13
							Compliment more (appearance, good meals, parenting, etc.).					
							Call during the day just to say hello.					
							Initiate conversation about the day's activities.					
							Give a "mini" massage.					
							Leave a love note.					
							Make coffee in A.M.					
							Take out garbage.					
							Help children with their homework.					

Make good eye contact when we speak.

Make activity suggestions for evening out.

Offer suggestions about my work problems.

Offer help with a chore.

Discuss my interests with me.

Express affection (holding hands, kissing, hugging, touching).

Kiss goodnight.

Wash my back when I'm in the shower.

day or two. The rewards, for those who persevere, are worth this initial effort. Commitment to the relationship is likely to increase; new, positive exchanges are likely to form on a gradual basis without the fear that usually accompanies more drastic change efforts; blaming and "I'll change after you" patterns will be weakened; and positive expectations and a renewed optimism will be generated.

THE PRINCIPLE OF TRUST

The Principle of Trust: One of the essential ingredients in an intimate relationship is the ability to count on our partner to not deceive and to behave in a way that promotes satisfaction and a sense of security.

Nothing is more terrifying than feeling we are losing control over our lives. This fear is common today, and for good reason: Unemployment is uncommonly high, the divorce rate is soaring, the economy is volatile, and the threat of nuclear confrontation clouds the future. As we lose control over these sectors of our lives (or discover we never really had control), we wish all the more to be secure in our intimate relationships and family life. If conditions are unstable elsewhere, having a trusted ally, a confidant, a person who will comfort and console, becomes all the more important.

To trust in another requires the absence of deceit, consistent and dependable behavior, and confidence that the other individual will act decently and with good intentions. Trust doesn't reside *within* a person (as a trait does); it is developed *between* people as a result of their experiences together. If A's behavior is consistent, unambiguous, and honest, B will feel trust because he or she can depend on this behavior. In contrast, deceit, pretending that things are a particular way when they are not, or saying one thing and acting in a contrary manner undermines feelings of trust.

Of all the deceptions to which romantic relationships are prone, it is probable that, as detailed in my book *The Other Man, The Other Woman*, the most dramatic and disruptive involves infidelity. Here again, what underlies the severe anxiety accompanying a mate's extramarital involvement is fear of the loss of control: control over our spouse, the relationship, the future, ourselves. There is also a fear of the loss of our partner's emotional bond, of the love, affection, and support we counted on. This can seriously weaken or destroy a relationship; by eroding if not entirely bankrupting trust, a discovered infidelity, can awaken frightening feelings of insecurity and loneliness. One woman, now divorced, describes her experience:

"I was going to a male psychologist at the time, and I remember telling him I thought my husband was seeing other women. He kept asking me why I was so untrusting and insecure. He confused me, and my husband confused me. Yet I was right after all. My instincts weren't wrong. I found out through my husband's diary that he *was* having affairs. He was also seen with her at a restaurant we frequently eat at. I was appalled. I begged him to stop. I carried on. I screamed, 'If you loved me, you wouldn't do this!' I ranted and raved and thought I was going to have a nervous breakdown. It took a long time for me to calm down. I felt like killing him; and at one point, I even got up to get a kitchen knife. I was frightened, frightened I might turn it on myself. During the course of the night, he made a clean breast of a whole lot of things he'd been doing over the past years: different women, women in his office, old friends of ours, business associates, and that sort of thing. He said none of it, no one person, had been important to him. And he swore he'd change, give it all up. I believed him; it sounded as if he were honest. I assumed my crying and misery had had an impact on him.

"He was very apologetic; and during the next year, he kept bringing home gifts for me, and he was generally more thoughtful than he'd ever been. I was flattered, reassured, and I began to relax. Then there was this night when we were driving by his office after a movie, and he suggested we go up and make love on the rug. I found that very romantic. It was a Saturday night, the building was dark and empty. I felt as if this was a clandestine kind of thing and was very excited. I really got into a whole fantasy about it. After we made love and had gotten dressed, he went into the bathroom. He was taking a really long time, and I was sitting behind his desk waiting for him. After a while, I opened a drawer, and staring me in the face was a letter that started out, 'To my lover.' Just then I heard him come out of the bathroom, so I grabbed the letter and put it in my pocket. When he came over to embrace me, I maneuvered around him saying I had to go now: 'It must have been something we ate.' In the bathroom I read the letter. I was shocked.

"The letter was from a woman he worked with. It was a love letter. She described her feelings about an evening they had spent together the previous week. I remember the night. I had felt lonely and wanted his companionship. He had told me he had a dinner date with a potentially important customer from out of town. 'It's one of those things,' he had said. The bastard! The letter mentioned me. This woman said she was jealous of me; she couldn't stand separating from him. She wanted him all for herself. She described some very private moments they shared. I felt as if someone had cut me open and pulled out my insides. Never have I felt so exposed, so vulnerable, so betrayed. I trusted him; he had promised to stop a year ago when I was so distressed, but even then he wasn't honest. I threw up. After a while, I came out of the bathroom; and although I was shivering all night as if I was in shock, I didn't let on I knew anything."

Infidelity, loosely defined, is a breach of trust. Although it is the sexual transgression that captures most of the attention in our society, distrust and deception occur more often, if not as dramatically, in the nonsexual aspects of a relationship. Robert maintains his friendship with Glen, an old army buddy, in utter secrecy. His wife, Dorothy, has always disliked Glen and has asked Robert not to see him. Robert has agreed but is undeterred. "I find a way," he says. "All Dorothy knows is that I'm working late, running an errand or the like. We go for a drink, hang out together, that sort of thing. If I told Dorothy, she would raise the roof, so why aggravate her?"

Then there's the partner who buys jewelry, an item of clothing, a decorative piece for the house, and instead of revealing the real price of the purchase, says, "I bought it at a sale," trimming the actual cost considerably. Gambling and drinking are also notorious forms of deception. Seldom do people who have some difficulty with these behaviors speak honestly of their losses or the extent of their drinking. Another hypocritical, trust-eroding practice involves the pretense of admiring the way a partner is dressed: "Oh yes, I think that jacket looks fine." "No, no, your stomach doesn't protrude in that skirt." Once again, the rationale is "I didn't want to hurt his (her) feelings."

Among the more sensitive areas, sex is a vital one in which to establish trust, and it is one in which small deceptions abound. How many women have kept the secret that they don't reach orgasms with their partners? Their reasons? They fake orgasms in order to bolster their partner's male ego and/or they are ashamed of their unresponsiveness. So long as the woman continues to pretend that she is orgasmic and her man continues to insist that she be, neither is building trust. Were the couple to discuss their dilemma honestly and discharge the myth that orgasm is the ticket to self-worth, it is quite conceivable that sex could be transformed from an exercise in mutual deceit to an expression of tenderness.

All deceptive maneuvers sabotage the building of trust between a couple, and prevents them from knowing themselves and others. What's more, beyond the benevolent explanation of the deception ("for the other person's sake") is the deceiver's attempt to protect him or herself. By being deceptive, he avoids confrontations and can continue the gambling, drinking, or whatever; at the same time, he can no longer sustain an open, trusting relationship. It is also probable, in some instances, that the deceived partner either knows or intuitively suspects that the truth is not being told; consequently, an air of suspicion hovers over the relationship.

While it is apparent that trust will be drained by deception, the effect of inconsistency on trust is less obvious. For example, if a husband verbally tells his wife that she is the most important person in his life and that she is his top priority, yet his daily behavior communicates only selfishness, lack of consideration, and irritability, how is the wife to be trusting? He may sincerely believe that he cares deeply for her and his words may be very flattering, but his behavior speaks more forcefully and belies his words. If a wife tells her husband that she trusts him implicitly to handle their finances yet innumerable times voices her concern about expenditures, income, and bill payments, can the husband be expected to trust his wife's statement that she "trusts him"?

Building toward greater honesty and thus toward increased trust therefore involves not simply saying what one believes but also doing what one says. To be counted on, one must demonstrate consistency of behavior. Being predictable and consistent does not, however, preclude change. Indeed, a person who remains the same throughout a long-term relationship would be hard to take even for the most tolerant among us; the boredom would be overwhelming. If trust is to be maintained, it must be based on both partners' willingness to be open and above-board so that each knows where he or she stands with the other and can depend on what the other says, *even in changing circumstances*. One may not necessarily like what one's partner says or does, and there may be distress surrounding certain changes that are occurring; but if there is no deception, no betrayal of trust, change can be understood, adjusted to, or modified. Only then can change occur with the fear of the unknown minimized.

In addition to discussing the changes that each experiences, intimate partners would be wise to recognize that change is an inevitable accompaniment to aging and altered life situations. Frequently, partners in an intimate relationship mistakenly regard change as a breach of trust, a signal for suspicion: "But you always liked my hair short, you must be tired of me"; "How can you say you hate your job, you love it. You must be planning something"; "What do you mean you don't want to go to the theater, you love ballets. What are you up to?" It is the failure to accept a partner as changeable that sets a person up for disappointment, that lays groundwork for him or her to conclude "I can't trust you."

Trust, then, is *not* based on a vow of sameness: "I hereby agree that I will always believe and behave exactly the way I did the day we met." In a vital, growing relationship, the vows will account for change. In *The Mirages of Marriage* Lederer and Jackson offer this statement as a foundation for trust between intimates: ". . . We are human beings, and will grow and change with age and circumstances. Neither of us is perfect. We are not afraid of being fallible and therefore we will be honest and open with each other, and reveal ourselves and our changes and failures. . . . If what happens is joyful (as we have faith it will be most of the time), we will treasure this good fortune. But if events are painful or harmful, we will adjust and accept the changes because it is a fact. Instead of being punitive toward each other, we will be consoling and encouraging. . . ."

Corrective Prescription

One cannot manufacture trust; it develops *as a result* of certain behavior, it is a consequence of honesty and consistency. An individual can choose to be honest and say what he experiences and what he feels; by acting in this way, he indicates that he can be trusted. Although honesty does not always bring a loving response, it is essential for it to occur. Herewith are several suggestions and experiments aimed at increased interpersonal honesty and consistency, and hence at building trust.

1. Partners in a relationship are entitled to rely on each other's promises or agreements. That is one of the foundations of trust. When spouses agree to behave in a particular way, failure to do so is a serious matter. Given the fact of human fallibility, don't promise more than you feel you are able to deliver. If you do, take the early initiative to discuss your misjudgment and renegotiate the agreement rather than going along with a pretense.

2. Consider the thoughts and experiences about which you are most ashamed/embarrassed. Pretend someone else has confessed these things to you. What counsel would you offer that person? Are you more benevolent toward this "other person" than toward yourself? Demonstrate confidence in your partner by discussing one or more of these experiences with him or her.

3. Keep a small notebook with you each day for a full week. Jot down each and every evasion, no matter how petty (for example, complimenting someone falsely, smiling when you're actually annoyed, telling people what they want to hear). Study the notebook at the end of each day to determine patterns of inauthenticity. Share these deceptions with your spouse and make a commitment to gradually change your behavior.

4. To trust another person, you must have trust in yourself. If you can count on your inner strength, you will be more willing to risk the vulnerability that comes with trusting others. Discuss your fears of vulnerability with your partner.

Trust is something that is worked out with considerable effort, often by taking two steps forward and one step back. But when it is achieved, trust itself can become a way of dealing with other relationship problems. If truthful disclosure encourages the growth of trust, trust in turn encourages the kind of disclosure that is needed for growth.

THE PRINCIPLE OF ACCEPTANCE

The Principle of Acceptance: A sound relationship permits expressions of anger, childishness, and silliness, as well as affection, without danger of condemnation. Thus, we can be as we really are, weak when we feel weak, scared when we feel confused, childish when the responsibilities of adulthood become overwhelming.

While most of us want to be loved and respected by our partners, we also fear that we may be found undesirable. For some people, this fear of rejection results in the formation of a false front, a mask to avoid being known. Hidden behind this mask is usually the belief, conscious or unconscious, that to be one's real self is dangerous, that exposure of real feelings will lead to being unwanted: "If my spouse really got to know me, he (she) wouldn't want any part of me." Consequently, a good deal of the stress and strain of the human condition comes from our striving to be something we are not; many of us fail to accept ourselves as fallible and, therefore, far-from-perfect human beings. Likewise, our failure to accept our partners, warts and all, is a significant source of relationship distress.

We all need opportunities to let our hair down, to be weak, to be sad, to be childish, to be crazy, sometimes, somewhere, with someone. That place is at home, with an intimate. Relationships that cease to provide sanctuary are those in which weaknesses are used as weapons, so that acting "out-of-character" is quickly suppressed. Arnold doesn't acknowledge Pam's existence unless she behaves in a certain way. The desired behavior is not clearly defined, although Pam knows that what Arnold wants—"an undemanding housewife who is efficient and charming"—isn't always how she feels. When Pam insists on being herself, which is sometimes needy, inefficient, and not so charming, she is told by Arnold, "You're mistaken. You're not the way you think you are. I know you. Deep inside you really are an undemanding housewife."

In some instances, the tactics of intolerance and nonacceptance go beyond denying or discounting part of an intimate's being and, instead, take the form of a direct attack at a sensitive area. Nina and Don are both in their early thirties and have been married for eight years. Nina is pregnant with their second child, and they are planning to move from their apartment into a house. Don is hard-working and earnest; however, as a young consulting engineer with very little business experience, he has suffered some serious financial setbacks.

Nina: That house in Lakeside is perfect for us. The location is first-class—we'll be making a great investment.

Don: It does have lots of nice qualities, but I'm afraid that the asking price, combined with the current mortgage rate, makes it out of reach for us.

Nina: Well, have you seen something that is more affordable?

Don: Yes, the houses in Davisport are larger, the taxes are lower, and the prices are within reason.

Nina: Are you kidding? That area is nowhere. Who would want to live there?

Don: What do you mean? We both grew up there. It's a solid, stable, middle-class area with good schools and services.

Nina: [beginning the attack] We could easily have afforded the house in Lakeside if your consulting firm hadn't collapsed.

Don: Oh, Nina, don't rub it in.

Nina: If you were more competitive, you would not have

lost so many potential clients to other firms. Now you seem to have given up. Working for someone else isn't going to produce any real money.

Don: I admit I made a few mistakes, that's why I'm learning more about the business. Listen, Nina, I feel bad enough . . .

Nina: A few mistakes? Hell, am I to be tied to a third-rate flunky who can't even hold a business together, who can't even provide a nice home for his family?

Don: Davisport homes *are* nice . . .

Nina: Look, we're going to buy the house in Lakeside. I'll ask my father for the money. I'll explain to him how you've made mistakes and that sort of thing; he'll loan us enough for a large down payment, and then even you will be able to keep up with the mortgage.

Don: Nina, you know it's important to me not to take money from your parents. You've done this before, disregarding my feelings; we'll take the house in Lakeside, I'll pick up some freelance work in the evenings to cover the extra cost.

Nina: [having effectively crushed Don's self-esteem] I knew you would work it out. I'll call the real-estate agent and make the arrangements.

There are those individuals who castigate their partners or make subtle (and sometimes harsh) judgments if he or she does not conform to expectations. In striking contrast is the individual who is self-accepting and who consequently has the strength and understanding to tolerate the foibles of another. Keith, a forty-eight-year-old high school English teacher was fortunate to become involved with such an individual. He had been divorced three months when he met Helen, a woman with whom he developed a stormy but ultimately positive relationship.

"When I met Helen, one of my strongest and most persistent feelings was pain—not just emotional pain but actual physical pain: nausea, headaches, and the like. I remember saying once that when my wife left me for another man and I lost the connection to my family, it was as if a knife were put into me and turned around each day to cut up my insides. My first reaction to Helen was one of surprise at her sensitivity and awareness of what and how I was feeling, even when I expressed it inarticulately or hardly at all. Then I began to get the feeling that not only was she sensitive but that she also cared about me. It seems crazy, but I fought desperately against this. I was firmly convinced that to give in to her acceptance of me meant selling my soul; there would be a high price for allowing another person into my life. Indeed, I was still reeling from the last time I yielded.

"I tried demonstrating to her how unworthy I was—how selfish, inadequate, nasty. I tried hating and attacking her. I told her that she couldn't possibly think well of me, that I was defective. I suggested that she was being deceitful and cruel to pretend that she accepted me. But she was always there, treating me with respect; she was a firm, strong pillar that I beat on to no avail and that merely said, 'You are a worthwhile human being.' She saw past my bullshit, yet she didn't condemn me for it. Not that she was a saint; she expressed anger, outrage, and frustration. She engaged me and fought ferociously, but she always did so in a way that didn't belittle me. Her words were strong yet soft; somehow the sharp edges were removed. She conveyed that I was not an obnoxious person but a person acting in an obnoxious manner. In other words, I was not disqualified and considered garbage because of my difficulties.

"As I look back on it now, I was putting all my faults and inadequacies on the line so that I could be done with the process of rejection. And Helen calmly (and sometimes not so calmly), by her acceptance of me as a person, peeled off my armor layer by layer. Slowly, it became clear that it was safe; I realized that I am the one who makes the ultimate judgment of my worth. That sounds like a simple, common-sense statement. Yet my appreciation of that dictum has given me such a sense of peace that it is awesome. I feel elevated, freer, accepting not only of myself but also of others. In my relationships with other people, I try to see them as individuals struggling with the same things as I do, not as adversaries or enemies. Most of us want the same things in our relationships: honesty, a sharing of feelings and thoughts, empathy, support, fun. Keeping these things in mind, my tolerance for others has expanded and my relationships, as a result, are much richer."

It should not be construed from the foregoing that acceptance is the same thing as liking. Obviously, we may not like all that another person is, but by acceptance we acknowledge and respect the fact that he or she is still worthwhile. It is this attitude that expresses "I may not like some of your behavior patterns, but that doesn't make you less of a person." People willing to reach out to others with this attitude can accept and tolerate differences without condemning the individual. They are wise to the human struggle and consequently, when another person behaves negatively, an attempt is made to understand the basis for this action. Aware of their own defenses, they are able to see through those of others without feeling personally attacked. Being accepted in this manner is something we can get, in varying degrees, only from our interpersonal relationships with wise parents, good friends, and some educators. It is endemic to some love relationships. And it is precisely this feeling of being valued that promotes our fullest functioning with an intimate.

Corrective Prescription

When an individual looks at another with a view toward making him or her into something new and different, a modern Pygmalion, it is probable that resentment will be engendered on both parts. The recipient often feels "not good enough," a rather unpleasant state, and the "helper" feels unfairly rebuffed in his or her efforts to "improve" his or her spouse. The following exercises represent an attempt to avoid this relationship contaminant by increasing acceptance of one's partner *as is*. It is not being suggested that change is unwelcome, only that change is unlikely when an individual feels under siege. The premise is that one must feel valued in order to have firm footing to move, to evolve further as a person.

1. Compose a list of the major criticisms you have about your partner. Now, sit down facing your spouse and reverse roles. Take turns speaking *as if you were your partner*, and express his or her feelings about one of the items on your list. Get into the role and present as thorough an understanding of this issue as possible from your partner's point of view. For example, a husband playing his wife might take an item from his list of complaints about her and say, "I'm really tired after a full day's work, cooking dinner and putting the children to bed. I know you get annoyed if I fall asleep early, so I try my best to stay up. Sometimes, though, I'm so exhausted I just can't make it." Try to really get into the experience of being your partner and understanding things from his or her viewpoint. Continue alternating until each of the criticism lists has been completed.

The ability to be compassionate toward a partner begins with attempting to understand him or her. Take at least a half hour to discuss your experience of this. What did you learn about your partner? About yourself? See if you can get into passionately defending your partner's (as well as your own) right to be fallible. Remind yourself of your acceptance equation when you are feeling intolerant of your partner: being human = being fallible.

2. Human beings are great "should makers." We are sufficiently egotistical to believe that because we would prefer something to occur, it *should* occur. The behaviors we view as more desirable in our partner *should* replace those deemed less desirable. Seldom do we stop to think, "Whoever guaran-

teed us that the world (our world, our family members) was designed to conform to our demands?" In the acceptance exercise below, we will increase our awareness of the absurdity of the "should" rule.

Each partner is to alternate beginning a sentence with "You should——" and complete the statement with a demand that your spouse be different. For example, "You should be neater!" It is very important that as you express your "should," you take the role of a parent scolding a child. Raise your voice, talk down to your partner—literally, by standing up and hovering over him or her, pointing your finger, and scowling. Do you feel somewhat like a nagging parent with your spouse? Now face each other, make good eye contact, and touch each other. Say the following sentence to each other, and pause to absorb what you experience as you do this: "I may not like some of your behaviors, but I value you overall, as an individual."

3. Sadly, many of us are caught up in negativism, so much that we are more alert to unpleasant occurrences than to pleasant ones. Some positive occurrences are taken for granted, some are minimized or even misunderstood, and occasionally some are silently noted. Too infrequently we express appreciation. It is likely that most of us would like to hear statements of appreciation more often—the objective of this last exercise.

Sit facing your partner, and take turns beginning a sentence with "I appreciate——" and go on to state your appreciation in sufficient detail so that your partner has a good sense of what it is that you find pleasing. Take about five minutes to do this. If you get stuck, just begin the sentence "I appreciate——," maintain good eye contact with your partner, and see what words come to you. Allow ample time to discuss how you felt as you gave and received appreciation. Be sure to include in your discussion the topic "how I can bring my appreciation of you into our daily living." Conclude the discussion when both of you have offered at least one viable suggestion for increasing expressions of appreciation.

It is important to note that being accepting does not mean a total subordination of one's own ideas, values, and desires. Criticism is part of all close relationships. Unlike those associations that do not involve intense emotion, however, criticism can be very potent, it can destroy as well as enhance. But it can be enhancing only if it is offered with understanding and proper timing. The intent, ideally, is to help improve a situation and add to a person's growth, not to tear down or cause unnecessary pain.

THE PRINCIPLE OF ALONE AND TOGETHER

The Principle of Alone and Together: Intimate relating involves an interdependence between partners who maintain their own individuality. Pleasing relationships are formed by people who desire to be together but do not *need* each other; each can function well alone.

When Alec was a youngster he was extremely shy and talked so low that he could hardly be heard. He had few friends; and because he felt quite uneasy among his peers, he did not participate in group activities. Alec shrank from actual physical contact with others; and when he was teased or rebuffed, he smiled weakly and backed away. As an adolescent, Alec didn't date; and although his social avoidance was not nearly as extreme through college, it was not until his senior year that he established his first relationship.

When Alec met Marie, he was immediately attracted to her.

She seemed to provide the element missing from his life. Feeling awkward with people and especially unwilling to play the role of pursuing male that the "dating game" called for, Alec believed that in Marie his prayers were answered. A striking redhead of thirty-four, brisk and saucy in manner, and highly skilled as a computer analyst, Marie surrounded herself with an extensive network of friends and acquaintances. Initially, Marie mistook Alec's shyness and social avoidance as evidence that he was a man at peace with himself, a man who could stand alone, a good listener and someone she could rely on. As for Alec, his anxieties about dating were quieted with Marie; she did most of the talking, took the initiative, and made most of the decisions.

Alec and Marie saw each other constantly for three months, fell very much in love, and were married. Without so much as a word of discussion, very early in their relationship they set up a pattern that eventually drove them apart. Throughout their courtship and marriage, Marie stopped seeing her friends; at Alec's request, they always did things as a couple, to the exclusion of their own interests. In effect, individual desires were discouraged by Alec, and only those actions that were mutually pleasing were accepted. Marie, viewing this lifestyle as a respite from the hectic social life she was used to, went along—temporarily.

During the second year of their relationship, Alec remained content with the togetherness arrangement, but Marie began to feel closed in and wanted more privacy, more time to pursue her interests and increased social contacts. Alec, resenting Marie's individuality and feeling threatened by it, became very critical of her. Marie grew impatient and angry, and started seeing her friends despite Alec's protests.

Three years of this escalating cycle—Marie wanting more independence, Alec demanding more togetherness—resulted in a relationship where resentfulness, despair, and bitterness had replaced the original ecstasy. There was no real communication, and whatever feelings they had once had for each other had been soured by Alec's dependency. Shortly after the third year of their marriage, they were divorced.

Marriage, or any committed relationship, cannot meet all the needs of an individual. Excessive dependence on another person diminishes our own capabilities and resourcefulness; instead of growth, stagnation, boredom, and resentfulness become the norm.

This is not to say that dependency plays no part in a relationship. All human beings are dependent; and a newborn infant is among the most helpless of all, needing other people —parents or parent surrogates—for its very survival. The parent must provide food and arrange the environment so that the child will stay alive, relatively free from pain, and be able to grow. As the child develops physically so that he or she becomes capable of greater learning, he or she will need others to emulate. The child needs to hear people talk, for example, so that he or she can learn to speak. He or she needs, in the early days of life, lots of contact—caressing, holding, and social stimulation. There is abundant evidence that without such close contact, the child's physical and psychological development will be impaired.

As adults, we are dependent on others for the exchange of goods and services, as well as for companionship and emotional gratification. We are, by nature, communal, and we rely on our ability to communicate and relate to our fellows. Experimental isolation studies demonstrate that long periods of seclusion from other living creatures tend to produce hallucinations and other pathological symptoms. It seems that just as tissues need oxygen, our psychic processes require contact and involvement with other people. Not that periods of separation from others are dangerous to one's well-being; indeed, there is evidence that the most integrated personalities need and actively seek solitude in order to contemplate and to discover their authentic feelings and beliefs.

While dependency is a healthy and natural part of the life

process, it can be corrupted, it can become excessive. We all know this, but some of us find it difficult to accept, especially when we want our partner's company and he or she has other plans. This refusal to accept another person as an individual free to see friends or to pursue independent interests will generally reflect poorly on a relationship.

Dysfunctional, relationship-eroding dependency is found among people who have lost touch with their values and their strength. Consequently, they need other people to lean on, to provide them with a sense of wholeness, and to reassure them by means of approval that they can function. It is as if self-esteem were not contained within the person but were contingent upon the judgment of others. This kind of person will often feel unable to tolerate being alone, since being in his or her own company is like being in the company of nobody.

In the dependent or "overintegrated" relationship, growth and development are stifled rather than enhanced. The relationship is overworked, overloaded, and there is an insistence that an undue degree of emotional support be provided. Here, the relationship affinity is so engulfing that both partners have lost their identities and uncomfortably share one confining identity as part of a couple. Neither partner can see any action by the other as casually separate from the self. If one member complains about something, the immediate response is "That's because you. . . ." Both bring each other into personal deliberations to an extreme that permits neither separation nor analysis of individual desires. Often, one party in the relationship begins pulling the other down, and a negative cycle is the result: Each one's negative qualities or attitudes feed the other's, creating a diminishing spiral that can destroy the relationship.

While too much dependency and emotional neediness can drain a relationship, too little togetherness can create a void, which gradually will weaken the connection between a couple. In the excessively autonomous or "underintegrated" relationship, the partners are far apart on most issues. They have vastly different interests, their life goals are divergent, and neither provides the other with desired companionship; there is more separateness than is suitable for at least one of the partners. Some individuals, in fact, are threatened by the commitment of a close relationship; they fear losing their freedom and overreact in a misguided effort to maintain their autonomy. One such individual, Carl, is twenty-eight and has been married for five years.

"When my wife was in her sixth month of pregnancy, it hit me: I'm stuck; I'm really married. We had been married for several years, but I never felt trapped or as if I was really married. There were no real responsibilities. With a child coming, I felt really scared. Was I doing the right thing? Was marriage really for me? Up until then, I had never really had to consider those questions. I guess in the back of my mind I always figured I could get out. With the pregnancy, I saw it was too late. What kind of heel would leave his wife in her sixth month? I couldn't live with that, but I also felt, for the first time, really tied down. What a lousy sense of timing. When Cathy flew to Minnesota to visit her aunt, I remember thinking maybe the plane would crash and I'd be free. It was a horrible thought. I was doing a lot of bickering, but I always considered Cathy a friend, a very decent, giving, and accommodating person. I was beside myself. . . .

"I began to avoid spending time with her. My activities, and there were plenty—golf, running, overtime at work, hanging around with buddies, burying myself in the TV—made the statement, 'I am an individual and I don't want to have to answer to anybody, I want to freely do my own thing.' My attitude was unreasonable, but, of course, I didn't see it then. In retrospect, I think three things were operating. I was threatened by the loss of my individuality; I really do have many tempting interests, and it was hard to restrict myself; I resented not being able to compete on the job or athletic field because I couldn't give it my all. It took me several years to work those things out. In the main, it finally became clear to me that individuality was at least, in part, a state of mind. When I felt I needed Cathy's permission to be my own person, I resented it; when I gave *myself* permission, I no longer felt resentful or rebellious."

It seems that too little togetherness may be a result of one partner's feelings of vulnerability, of fear of losing him or herself in the relationship; or it may be a product of incompatible interests or goals, hidden resentments, or differing needs for closeness. On this last issue, some people naturally have a higher need of affection, companionship, and shared activities. Others prefer pursuing individual interests with a passion. In any case, the closeness of courtship and the enthusiasm of a new relationship usually mask any differences along the alone-together continuum. However, these types of differences, if present, can generate acute distress unless they are reconciled early in the relationship.

Corrective Prescription

The amount of time individuals spend with their partners and the degree of dependency on each other vary from couple to couple. The fact is that relationship congeniality depends not so much on the amount of time a couple actually spend together or apart as it does on whether they *agree* on how to make that allocation. As for dependence, this is an important issue for individuals and couples, yet it does not easily lend itself to measurement. What is too much? What is too little? Again, individual needs vary, and whether or not the degree of dependency is troubling will be determined by the degree of compatibility between the people involved. A fiercely independent individual, for example, is not likely to admire, respect, and live harmoniously with a deeply dependent individual. Change during the course of the relationship is also an important factor. One partner may want more (or less) separateness than was previously the case. Once more, this becomes a problem only if it is incompatible with the desires of the other partner.

Since the issues discussed above require individualized application, it is suggested that couples begin by discussing the together-alone aspect of their relationship in detail: When your partner pursues an independent interest or activity, do you feel abandoned or neglected? Does your partner's alone time convey: "I don't like you and therefore wish to be independent of you"? Do you feel apologetic if you want to be alone? To what extent do you rely on your partner to do things you are uneasy about doing? (This often involves issues of assertiveness: "Dear, would you call the Smiths and tell them we can't make it? You know how I hate to reject people.") What types of interests and activities have you developed that you can call your own? What kind of behavior emanating from your partner would enhance your time together? In what way, if any, does your partner inhibit your individuality?

The exercises that follow are geared toward helping you appreciate aloneness and company, as well as the related issues of dependence-independence. Based on the prior discussion with your partner, sample those activities that provide balance for you. If you are heavy into alone time, for example, select companionship activities; if you are uncomfortable relying on your partner, experiment with being more dependent. If you lean too heavily on your partner, select those activities that promote self-reliance.

1. Choose several places you normally go only when accompanied by someone and go to each of these places alone.

2. Invite your partner to accompany you to those activities you usually go to alone.

3. Make a date to go out with yourself one night each week for two consecutive weeks. Plan the evening so that it is stimu-

lating and challenging. Don't spend the time in front of a television set.

4. Make a date to go out with your partner one night each week for two consecutive weeks. Go someplace where you are able to spend at least some time talking intimately to each other.

5. Ask your spouse to do you a favor. Do not make this a superficial request; it should involve something personal.

6. Push yourself to do something you normally have your partner do for you. This should be an activity about which you are uneasy or fearful. It may include taking the initiative in planning an activity, carrying the conversation in a social gathering, or turning down an invitation.

7. For the next week, try to make as many household and personal decisions as you can alone. If you ordinarily do this, experiment with consulting your partner more often before making decisions.

Discuss your experiences with the exercises above. Ask your partner what you can do to further his or her enjoyment of time spent together and apart.

THE PRINCIPLE OF KEEPING IN TOUCH

The Principle of Keeping in Touch: There is a hunger for body contact within all of us; tactile stimulation in the form of caressing, fondling, cuddling, embracing, stroking, and the like is a crucial relationship resource.

In his wonderful book *Touching*, Ashley Montagu suggests consulting a dictionary for the various meanings of the word *touch* to provide a clue to the importance of this sensory experience. It is, for example, far and away the longest entry—fourteen full columns—in the authoritative *Oxford English Dictionary*. Originally derived from the Old French *touche,* the word is defined by the *Oxford English Dictionary* as "the action or an act of touching (with the hand, finger, or other part of the body); exercise of the faculty of feeling upon a material object." The key word, Montagu points out, is *feeling*. Although touch itself is not an emotion, touching and being touched can be powerful acts and are often experienced emotionally.

Despite the desirability and perhaps because of the potency of touching, it is often neglected in relationships. It seems that in this age of computers and impersonal contact, too many of us have become "programmed" to avoid touching or to confine it to a few permissible circumstances such as sex, athletics, casual greetings, and aggressive expressions. This is highlighted by the results of an experiment conducted by Professor Kenneth Gergen and his colleagues of the Department of Psychology at Swarthmore College. These researchers found that when persons were introduced into a pitch-black room in which there were half a dozen strangers, persons they knew they would never meet again, more than 90 percent touched each other on purpose and nearly 50 percent hugged each other. In contrast, almost none of the participants in a similar group made any sort of tactile contact in a lighted room.

The experimenters were struck by the desire of their dark-room subjects to make contact; given anonymity, a group of perfect strangers moved very rapidly (about thirty minutes) to a stage of intimacy seldom attained in years of casual socializing. It was concluded from these findings that people share strong yearnings to be close to each other, but that our social norms discourage us from expressing these feelings physically: "Don't touch him (her); he (she) may get the wrong idea."

Surprisingly, the idea that tactile stimulation is desirable, even necessary, for well-being has gained recognition only in recent years. When the results of psychologist Harry F. Harlow's ground-breaking experiments on infant monkeys were published in 1958, the subject of touching—especially the warm comfort of a mother's touch—came under close scientific scrutiny. Briefly, what Harlow did was supply newborn monkeys with two surrogate mothers: one warmed with a light bulb and covered with a soft terry cloth, the other merely a bare wire frame. The monkeys were divided into two groups, one given a nursing cloth mother, the other given a nursing wire-frame mother.

Dr. Harlow observed that the monkeys fed from the wire-framed mothers spent only enough time on those wire frames to stay alive. The rest of the time they spent clinging to the comforting cloth-covered mothers. Harlow wrote of the experiment: "We were not surprised to discover that contact comfort was an important basic affection or love variable, but we did not expect it to overshadow so completely the variable of nursing. . . ." In essence, Harlow found that his infant monkeys valued tactile stimulation more than they did nourishment, for they preferred to cling to "mothers" who provided physical contact without nourishment to wire ones who did supply nourishment. Moreover, and perhaps most importantly, with deprived tactile stimulation, monkeys became nervous, awkward, irritable, and seriously impaired in their development.

There is little doubt that Harlow's findings have important implications for human beings. Babies need to be touched; without it, their development is likely to be impaired. In fact, as Dr. Montagu reports, during the nineteenth century and as late as the second decade of the twentieth century, a fascinating but quite tragic mystery surrounded infant death. The mortality rate for infants under one year of age in various institutions throughout the United States was nearly 100 percent. In one institution, since all babies admitted there and retained for any length of time died, it was customary to enter the condition of the child on the admission card as hopeless.

America at the time was profoundly influenced by Dr. Luther Holt, professor of pediatrics in New York. Dr. Holt, considered an unquestionable authority—the Dr. Spock of his time—dogmatically insisted that "tender loving care" spoiled the baby. Children's institutions consequently handled children minimally or not at all. Needless to say, this lack of handling, the tactile deprivation, was not suspected of being a mortality factor. It was not until several American pediatricians influenced by the dramatically lower mortality rates in European institutions gained prominence that the death mystery was clarified. What the child needs if he or she is to thrive, it was found, is to be handled and carried and caressed and cuddled. After applying these findings in pediatric institutions, mortality rates dropped for infants under one year to less than 10 percent by 1938.

In adults, the need to be held, touched, and cuddled, like other needs, varies in intensity from person to person and in the same person, from time to time, but it is present in all of us. Dr. Marc H. Hollender of the Vanderbilt School of Medicine has studied women and their reactions to touch. From their research, Hollender and his co-workers believe that for some women the need to be held or cuddled is a major determinant of sexual behavior. In-depth interviews revealed that many women engage in sex with men when their real desire is to be held. As Hollender and his colleagues stated in the journal *Medical Aspects of Human Sexuality*:

> The desire to be cuddled and held is acceptable to most people as long as it is regarded as a component of adult sexuality. This wish to be cuddled and held in a maternal manner is felt to be too childish; to avoid embarrassment or shame, women convert it into the longing to be held by a man as part of an adult activity, sexual intercourse.

In a study of the wish to be held during pregnancy, Hollender and an associate found that in the majority of women, there was a distinct increase in the desire to be held; this was assumed to coincide with the desire for demonstrated reassurance. In some women, those who felt themselves to be physically unattractive, there was a decrease in the frequency of requests to be held. Such women, the investigators suggested, may have had a difficult time accepting physical affection because they felt unworthy, a consequence of their "poor" appearance. It may be interpreted by these findings that women are very much attuned to and desirous of touch, particularly during periods of vulnerability. Words are certainly important, but acts of touching that communicate affection and involvement are crucial.

As for men, Europeans have hugged and kissed each other for centuries. American men, in contrast, choose the more reserved handshake, the rugged slap on the back, or the poke in the ribs. Athletics are one of the few areas where men have permitted each other to touch and be touched, through the ritual of swats across the behind and bear hugs, without fearing that their image would be tainted by "unmanly" behavior. Indeed, in athletic settings—football, for instance—the sporting activity is considered so masculine that all doubt is cancelled. It is like saying, in effect, "I've got masculinity to spare. I am very sure of myself." Just as physical affection between men is masked by athletics or alcohol (picture the familiar scene of two drunks holding each other up), it is similarly disguised when relating to women. Here, sex becomes the major vehicle once again; hence, the familiar lament of many women, "He touches me only when he wants sex." Certainly, it would not be risky to venture that men as well as women long to be held and caressed without having to be sexually involved. It is apparent to most observers, though, that men have an even more difficult time than women acknowledging and satisfying their hunger for touch.

From Hercules to James Bond, the heroic man has been presented as impenetrable, unyielding, completely self-sufficient. Witness some discriminating reactions to male and female children: A shy little girl is considered cute; a shy boy is thought of as a sissy. A frightened girl is comforted; a boy is admonished to act like a man. Girls are allowed comfortably to kiss each other and to cry openly without shame; boys who even touch each other had better be "horsing around," and crying is done only at the expense of sheer ridicule.

These behavioral distinctions were confirmed in a recent study that revealed that the majority of surveyed parents did not hug or cuddle their sons (after the average age of five), would not kiss male children at all after a certain age (usually the onset of adolescence), and would discourage boys as young as four years old from sobbing by calling them crybabies or telling them to "act their age." When asked to explain the lack of physical affection and the prohibition against crying, the most common response from parents was, "I don't want my son to grow up to be a sissy."

Corrective Prescription

We have seen that the significance of touching is considerable. From the moment of birth, touch is fundamental to the development of human behavior. Moreover, couples who minimize physical contact—exclusive of sexuality—are in danger of "losing touch" with each other. Besides the pleasures and satisfactions that come from the feel of a loved one's skin, touching provides an emotional link between intimates. A compassionate touch can calm anxiety, ease pain, soothe fear, provide emotional security. Yet, our society, influenced as it has been by puritanical traditions, tends to discourage the reaching out and touching of one another.

Many of our inhibitions to touch are based on a concern with "image," with how it will look to somebody else. Men are particularly plagued by this image problem; women are, too, even if to a lesser extent. It may well be that after ignoring our desire for tactile contact, for a time, we are left with a vague sense of dissatisfaction—feeling out-of-touch—but we no longer recognize its source. Touch hunger, as with prolonged hunger for food, will eventually evaporate if not fulfilled. This does not mean that the requirement is gone, only that the "pump must be primed" in order to (literally) "bring us to our senses."

The suggestions that follow are intended to heighten our appreciation of touch, to increase relationship involvement, and to foster goodwill.

1. Each day, touch your partner in a nonsexual but intimate manner. This may include an embrace, a squeeze, an arm around the shoulder, caressing your partner's hand, and the like. A perfunctory peck on the cheek will not do; it is not a substitute for a warm embrace, nor is a conventional handshake capable of replacing a caressing hand.

2. For the next few days, try to keep track of when and how you touch and respond to touch during your daily routine. Talk about your findings with your partner.

3. When you meet a friend or relative whom you haven't seen in a while, touch and embrace him or her. Don't discriminate on the basis of sex.

4. With bare back, sit back to back with your partner, close your eyes, and silently focus your awareness on your back making contact with your partner's. Let your back begin to move a little and interact with your partner in a tactile conversation.

Continue to interact with your back and gradually bring your head, arms, and hands into the interaction. Let the movement flow freely and expressively. After about ten minutes, silently and slowly say good-bye with your body and bend slightly forward. Pause to reflect on the experience. Then turn around, face your partner, and share how you felt, what your partner's back was like, the intent of your touch conversation, and so on.

5. One evening a week, take turns caressing your partner's

entire body. Take a shower together, go to bed without clothes, and have the receiving partner lie on his (her) stomach.

The giving partner is to begin with the back of the head, ears, and neck, caressing gently and tenderly, then going down the back and sides, down the buttocks, inside the thighs, legs, and feet. A light, warm body oil may be used if desired

The receiver is to concentrate on his (her) feelings. This is very important. Don't worry about your partner becoming tired. Stay with *your* feelings, and give feedback during the experience only if something feels particularly pleasant or unpleasant. Otherwise, discuss the experience *after* it is over. At that time you can instruct your partner as to your touch preferences (lighter, harder, slower, faster) for future contacts.

After a while (usually twenty minutes or so), when the back of the body has been completed, the receiver is to turn over and the front of the body is done in the same way. Start with the head, face, and neck, slowly and gently and with sensitivity—as if you were blind and "seeing" with your fingers—moving to the chest, belly, and sides. Massage the thighs, legs, feet. As with the back, caress the front until you or your partner has had enough. Then change places; the giver becomes the receiver.

PART III

And What About Sex?

Of the many forms of intimacy—a smile across the room, a shared hardship, a family ritual, a kiss, a touch—sex is probably fraught with more confusion, unrealistic expectations, misunderstanding, and disillusionment than any other. Sex promises emotional fulfillment, security, reassurance, and intimacy, even if it often fails to deliver. For both men and women, the pressure to perform sexually adds a burdensome demand to their bond. The overemphasis on sexual technique of recent years—sex manuals have become as popular (and as disappointing, ultimately) as diet books—has resulted in men's and women's frantic efforts to be sexually with it.

Clinical exploration of sex and sexuality has vastly improved our sexual climate and washed away much ignorance and rigidity. But the concentration on sexual techniques and gimmicks, an offshoot of the sexual revolution, cuts off many couples from true intimacy. Caught up in the mechanics and methods of satisfying their partner, they lose sight of the most basic aspect of sexuality: the expression of feelings. A case in point involves the experiences of Joan and Martin, both of whom have had their share of disappointing relationships.

JOAN:

"The man in my last relationship never expressed any appreciation for me and rarely even kissed me. It was sex and no closeness. A few months of the same unaffectionate routine contaminated our sex life. Sex became a weapon in a power struggle. If I couldn't get him to respond to me as a person, to be tender and loving, I wasn't going to respond to him physically and emotionally. I started withholding sex or giving it and going through the motions in a perfunctory manner. I was saying directly and through sex: 'I want our relationship to be better—warmer, more feeling-oriented, less mechanical.' He was either threatened by that or he misunderstood, because he became very rigid and countered with, 'You're frigid; you have sexual hang-ups.' That was his favorite line. In my view, our sexual problems were really relationship problems that expressed themselves sexually. I think sex enjoyment is increased by how we act toward each other in all aspects of our lives together. Sex is part of the relationship; I don't see it as a separate entity."

MARTIN:

"I agree with Joan. I feel sex is an integral part of a relationship. That's what makes it so gratifying. When Joan and I first became physically involved, I went through a few months of fear about how good she would think my performance was and how I compared to her other lovers. I was particularly plagued by imagined comparisons to her former partner: 'Was she matching our abilities as lovers? Did I measure up to him in that regard?' I also came into the situation with a backlog of negative reactions from my last relationship. Maybe in some relationships the sex stays good even if the relationship doesn't. Not in mine. Sex became terrible, and we both traded barbs in that area. So sex with Joan—an important person in my life—was tense. I was giving myself a hard time from several quarters.

"One night something interesting happened that has had a very positive effect. Joan was feeling sexier than I was, and she came on to me. I had had a particularly grueling day and really wasn't in the mood for sex, but she snuggled up to me and I felt compelled to respond. Things didn't go too well, though. I couldn't get aroused; I wasn't able to get an erection. So I said to Joan, 'I'm sorry.' She looked at me with love and tenderness and said, 'Don't be sorry. You don't have to prove anything to me. I love you next to me, holding me, talking to me. You can touch me, kiss me. I love it! Our relationship is not going to be judged by erections!' From that time on my performance fears disappeared. Joan was right. Two people who are basically loving toward each other, who express good feelings toward each other, don't need to prove through sex that they're valuable people. All they have to do is relax and enjoy each other."

While there's no ready formula for connecting sexually, being able to "relax and enjoy each other," as Martin put it, certainly helps. In order to do this, a couple has to go beyond the physical experience; without the intimate exchange of thoughts, feelings, and desires, even the most fiery of sexual relationships will soon dry up. Feelings of closeness and distance cannot be divorced from sexual satisfaction and dissatisfaction; a couple's relationship out of bed cannot be separated from what happens to them in bed. In effect, sexual satisfaction often corresponds to the degree of non-sexual satisfaction within the relationship.

Although sex is only one link in the chain of relating intimately, it is, to most of us, invested with a great deal of importance. When one or both partners are sexually displeased, for example, it is not unusual for this displeasure to spill over into other areas of the relationship. With this in mind, let us turn to some factors which, in contrast to popular prescriptions for sexual acrobatics and gimmicks, seem to have wide applicability for sexual enhancement.

Perhaps the most important sexual principle is *enlightened self-interest*. Enlightened self-interest involves making love for yourself, first. In contrast to selfishness, which is based on "I want what I want regardless of anyone's feelings or inconvenience," enlightened self-interest is founded on the notion that you are entitled to seek pleasure as long as you are responsive to your partner's efforts to do the same. In seeking pleasure you are responsible for teaching your partner how to please you. You ask for what you want, and you tell (or show) your partner how to please you if he or she is not already doing so.

Not only is this approach to sex quite acceptable but, paradoxically, it usually increases your partner's pleasure. There is a delightful freedom in being with a person sexually—or nonsexually, for that matter—who can be counted on to look out for him or herself and to express his or her likes and dislikes. By communicating your enjoyment and taking responsibility for your sexual preferences, your partner can relax and concentrate on his or her *own* pleasure; that is, in the process of pleasing yourself, your enthusiasm and excitement not only stimulate your partner but free him or her to do the same.

It is not easy to follow the principle of enlightened self-interest; many of us have been brought up to be sexually shy and inhibited. During lovemaking it is not uncommon for a couple to be reluctant to signal each other, directly or indirectly, for a variety of reasons: embarrassment, fear, habit, lack of practice, or self-consciousness ("I don't want to admit that I like those things; I want them to just happen"). For better or worse, these kinds of things seldom "just happen." Each individual's source of stimulation is a highly personal and variable matter; maintaining a wall of silence around sexual feelings forces partners to make assumptions that may be incorrect—or correct one time and incorrect another. Even men and women with considerable sexual experience may fail to keep each other up-to-date about their sexual preferences.

Joyce and Peter are one such couple. Joyce had lived with a man for two years and had had a number of brief affairs prior to meeting Peter. Peter had been married for three years and had dated extensively after his divorce. When he met

Joyce, he had been single for three years and felt ready for another try at a committed relationship. Five months of dating convinced both Joyce and Peter to tie the knot. Besides their sexual attraction, they shared similar hopes and dreams, and felt very much in love.

After two years of marriage, Joyce's sexual interest began to gradually wane. Peter, disappointed, hurt, and confused, blamed marriage. "We never had any problem with sex before we married," he complained. When Joyce defended their decision to marry, Peter retorted by accusing her of faking sexual interest in order to "hook" him. The underlying difficulty was not the decision to marry, nor any pretense on Joyce's part to be sexually interested. In fact, she was quite disturbed by her diminishing sexual satisfaction with Peter.

Joyce and Peter's initial lovemaking had been inflamed by passion; the excitement of discovery, of novelty, had promised to spring their fantasies to life. It had been a glorious time when the hours sped by and the nights were never long enough. But this early sexual excitement soon cooled down. This was to be expected, although not to the extent that Joyce experienced it; there may be fewer sparks, but the fires usually aren't dampened completely! "Monotony," "the treadmill," "humdrum," are words that describe states of feeling from which most of us seek escape. This seems true whether tedium stems from working eight hours on an assembly line, eating the same food day after day, or going through the same sexual motions over and over. "Satiation" is the technical word for it; "fed up" is somewhat more descriptive. This is what Joyce was experiencing, and, actually, Peter was as caught up in it as Joyce. Their sexual experience had become routine.

Invariably Peter would indicate that he felt like having sex. Joyce would agree because she felt she should. Since Joyce was not as eager as she had been in the early days of their relationship, she was slower in becoming aroused—lubrication was insufficient—and Peter found entry difficult, while Joyce experienced discomfort. Peter remained silent about his lack of enjoyment; Joyce passively endured her displeasure. Mild complaints were occasionally exchanged ("If I didn't come on to you, we'd never have sex"; "I have other things on my mind; all you ever think about is sex!"), but the substance of their complaints remained untouched.

Specifics aside, this couple's plight is one that frequently occurs in an ongoing relationship. In brief, less novelty → less desire for lovemaking → more pressure to make each "performance" count → less enjoyable sex → even less desire → more resentment, increased performance concern → increased difficulty talking about it as the demoralizing cycle escalates. In contrast, a more positive cycle might look like this: less novelty → discussion of sensual feelings, fantasies, desires → sexual experimentation based on discussion → continued discussion (feedback) and experimentation, refinements → better sex → increased desire.

In the more positive sequence above, openness replaces secretiveness; experimentation and sexual variety replace rigidity and stagnation; pleasure replaces pressure and reinforces enthusiasm for sexual contact.

There are a number of other guidelines that couples can apply to enhance and express their mutual intimacy:

1. We plan almost everything in our lives—dental appointments, business meetings, luncheon dates, jogging—but how often do we set aside private, uninterrupted time on a regular basis for sex play? Instead of haphazardly snatching a chance for sexual intimacy, *schedule time* as you would for more "serious" pursuits, such as cleaning the house or watching a football game.

2. Each individual is the world's foremost authority on his or her sexual pleasure. And, as we have seen, it is each individual's responsibility to teach his or her partner how to be a better lover. Accordingly, make a list of sexual turn-ons and turn-offs to share with your partner. Include in your notes "atmosphere" elements (candlelight, music, etc.) and allow

your imagination to run wild. Position, practices, locales, can all be altered. Dare to break out of your routine.

3. Educate yourself sexually. Of course, facts alone aren't enough. Some couples who are experienced and knowledgeable continue to have an unrewarding sex life. Yet, others suffer needlessly because of inadequate or misleading information. Most adults today did not have the opportunity to review straightforward, authentic material about sexual expression as they matured. Only during the last fifteen years or so has realistic sex information become widely available. Prior to that time, sexual reading matter seemed to be primarily pornographic or written for a professional audience. There was no middle ground. A few examples of readable, reliable books include Nancy Friday's *My Secret Garden* (Trident Press, 1973); Albert Ellis's *The Sensuous Person* (New American Library, 1974); Bernie Zilbergeld's *Male Sexuality* (Little, Brown, 1978); Lonnie Barbach's *For Yourself: The Fulfillment of Female Sexuality* (Doubleday, 1976).

4. Many men and women find pleasure in varying degrees of physical contact in the form of cuddling, kissing, and holding, which do not have to lead to sexual intercourse. Stroking and being stroked, in fact, can develop an appreciation of how warm, rich, pleasing, and stimulating simple body contact can be. When you really get into allowing your *total* body to turn on, the genitals, more often than not, take care of themselves. In this regard, take the opportunity on several occasions to spend an hour or so in bed with your partner. There is to be no intercourse or direct genital stimulation. Instead, focus on the sensations that pass through you by touching, lying against each other in a variety of ways—rubbing backs, bellies, or toes—kissing, licking, moving, embracing.

5. Most men and women have experienced rigid sex-role training. For example, while men have been told that rough and tough is masculine, women have been told that soft and sweet is feminine. When men and women confine themselves exclusively to either "masculine" or "feminine" behavior, they

limit themselves and become incomplete human beings. Consequently, they have decreased freedom to express and act out a wider range of feelings and behavior.

To diminish these self-imposed limits and thereby increase your range of sexual satisfaction, spend several days "reversing" your sex roles attitudinally and expressively. If you are male and conceive of a woman as being gentle or seductive, cuddly or passive, sexually be that way yourself. If you are female and view men as aggressive, initiatory, active, you be that way. Be true to form in coming "out of role" in your sex play. For instance, if the female partner usually lies on her back and is mounted by the male, reverse this; if the male partner usually fondles his lover's nipples, she is to fondle his.

The suggestions above are not intended as panaceas. Some sexual problems, particularly if they are chronic—erectile failure, inability to achieve orgasm, premature ejaculation—warrant professional consultation. However, it is a myth that sex in a long-term relationship cannot continue to be fulfilling.

If *your* sex life seems to be foundering, examine your feelings and behaviors; look at your patterns of sexual expression. Do you communicate your feelings honestly? Are you actively involved in the relationship? Do you provide the daily praise of your partner that enhances nightly affection? Do you keep yourself vital, stimulating, and attractive as a person? What are you doing to transfer this vitality to your sexual behavior? It is quite likely that within your response to these questions you will find some directives for sexual and relationship enhancement.

PART IV

We Never Talk Anymore: Introduction to Communication Principles

Enduring relationships require that individuals supply one another with a great deal of pertinent information. In many relationships, though, an opposite process, one of restricted communication, occurs: "What he doesn't know won't hurt him." "The best thing may be not to tell her. Why bother my wife with professional or business issues she really doesn't understand?" "He has enough to worry about." It is not surprising that many letters to the advice-giving sages in the daily press deal with problems of this kind. There is an impressive research literature documenting the connection between satisfying relationships and good communication between partners. It shows rather conclusively that skillful communication is an essential element of an intimate relationship.

Men and women have always been sexually attracted to each other, and there is an extensive body of literature on sexual relations between intimates. But only very recently has there emerged an emphasis on good social relations between the sexes in long-term relationships. Most middle-aged adults grew up in households in which marital intimacy between their parents was not even considered an aspired goal. Against the plea for openness between husband and wife are pitted the

89

long-standing social facts of life: "If you talk too much you give yourself away. You give her (him) something to use against you." Deceptions and lies are almost institutionalized, standard operating procedures between the sexes. As a result, rather than sharing the closeness of an intimate relationship, many husbands and wives live in their very separate emotional worlds:

"Our meeting was absolutely beautiful and very romantic. Joseph was a blind date arranged through a mutual friend. I didn't ordinarily go on blind dates, but my friend really urged me on this one. She was right! We went to dinner but never noticed the food. We couldn't talk enough, we got misty-eyed again and again; we were so enraptured with each other. Joseph and I went back to his apartment, and we talked and made love almost all night. I had had plenty of relationships that were mostly sexual, but I knew this one was different, and so did Joseph. After three months, when he asked me to marry him, I wasn't surprised—it was natural and inevitable.

"The beginning of our marriage continued in the direction of our courtship; we both shared a sense of warmth, a feeling of being loved, a feeling of having taken out an option on a partnership. We felt very close. We told things to each other that we'd never confided in anyone else. Sometimes we'd lie in bed and talk into the small hours of the morning. The whole world seemed to spread out for us to explore together. But as open and intimate as we were in those early days of our relationship, just so closed and frozen did we become over the years. Now we have so little to say. Little by little we have bottled up our feelings—of both love and resentment—until we seem to feel nothing at all for each other.

"The intimacy seems to have gone out of our marriage. Our sense of each other, that deeply personal dimension, had been superb when we just met, but over the years it has faded and shrunk until our original ecstasy is no longer recognizable. We were simply too busy—he with his career, I with the responsibilities of our home and family—to notice that we were no longer connecting. He would retreat as soon as he came home —to the garage, where he worked on restoring an antique car, or into the den, where he built ship models. On those occasions when he was receptive or cheerful, I was resentful of all the times he wasn't, and spitefully did not make myself available. In return, when I took an initiative to talk he would demonstrate his disinterest by promptly falling asleep. After a while, conversation just about dried up. Now there is nearly a total lack of communication between us on our philosophy of life, goals, dreams, etc. On those rare occasions when we do talk personally, the conversation takes on an impersonal flavor. It seems contradictory to have an "impersonal" personal conversation, but somehow that's what happens. Mainly, though, we stick to safe topics: the weather, the children's clothing, and the price of food at the supermarket.

"The ironic thing about this is that my friends who knew us when we were enthusiastic about our relationship would always rib us about our nonstop talking. They would comment that going out with us felt like an intrusion, we were so taken by our own conversation that they hated to interrupt. That seems like a very long time ago; now we are together for the simple reason that we cannot endure the thought of living alone. I have cultivated a kind of existential resignation and wry humor about the whole thing: 'Don't take it all so hard,' I tell myself. 'All marriages are like this!' But in all honesty, I don't really believe that. There must be more to it. All the women's magazines, from *Redbook* to *Cosmopolitan*, always give the same advice: Stroke him, massage his ego, tell him what he wants to hear, pretend. That's such a bunch of nonsense. How can I have a 'repair' conversation based on dishonesty and deceit? It is difficult enough to be agonized by the void in our relationship. I am not about to add lies and deception to our comedy of errors. The problem is, at this stage of our relationship, how can I express my true feelings and needs in such a way that is not threatening or seen as blaming? Lately, I have felt that the real barrier between us, the basis of our fading relationship, has progressed beyond our inability to talk to each other. We have become strangers to each other's experiences of life."

Performing whatever duties are called for in a marriage—provider, parent, sex partner—is enough to make the relationship functional; it is not enough to ensure satisfaction. For that, skillful communication must be added to the marital stew. Without skill in a continuum of abilities ranging from the sending of information to the reception and interpretation of information, individuals are unable to make explicit what they expect of each other, what is agreeable and what is not. Monitoring which experiences are bonding and which are alienating, understanding each other's habits and hang-ups, and effecting a coupling that achieves the "we" while protecting the integrity of the "you" and "me," become impossible when communication is sorely deficient.

And herein lies a major basis for relationship failure. While it is fashionable nowadays to complain about "communication problems," many couples—influenced by the folklore of romantic love—believe that an innate sensitivity should link them and their partner. Being in a relationship, some contend, affords them the privilege of being less diligent in their efforts to communicate than they might be in their casual contacts. In effect, they say, "You ought to know how I feel or what I mean if you really love me." Unfortunately, this is often *not* the case. One of the most thought-provoking results of the considerable research done in this area is how little husbands and wives really do know or understand one another. "I know him (her) like the back of my hand," brags a husband or wife. Yet, under experimental conditions, their performance more closely resembles the comical, embarrassingly inaccurate mates of the "Newlywed Game" than teammates who correctly assess each other's signals.

Even in the simplest kind of predictions of one another's behavior, couples are usually wrong. In a report published in

Marriage and Family Living, researchers asked spouses which one of them would tend to talk more during a decision-making process dealing with how they would spend a hypothetical gift of several hundred dollars. The session was recorded so that the actual amount of talking done by each could be measured. Only seventeen out of fifty individuals correctly calculated who would be the more active negotiator. What's more, after the session was over and the participants were again asked who had talked more, over half still judged incorrectly!

In another study, investigators increased the participants' motivation to forecast correctly by presenting an assortment of items—gloves, scarves, lingerie, belts, wallets—some suitable for men, some for women. If, without communication, they could successfully coordinate their choices—that is, choose the same item—they would receive the items as rewards. They all failed. Not one of the twenty-five participating couples succeeded in predicting one another's choices on as many as five of all twenty items.

In still another study, this time involving 116 couples, each partner was asked separately to give the names of persons considered by both spouses to be close mutual friends, not including relatives. In an astonishing result, only six couples were in total accord on this task, while one couple were in complete disagreement regarding their mutual friends.

Not surprisingly, couples who have a solid, communicative relationship understand each other better than those who are unhappily married. One study of eighty-two happily married couples and eighty unsatisfactorily married couples revealed that nearly three-quarters of the former but less than half of the latter couples agreed in their checking of an elaborate 128-item questionnaire concerned with their perceptions of themselves and of their spouses. It may be, of course, that husbands and wives have a good understanding of each other because the marital relationship is communicative to begin with, or they may enhance their communication because they have a good understanding of each other, or both. Whatever the direction of the association, however, a major feature in relationships lacking in intimacy is a deficiency in communication skills; in discordant relationships, there is a marked failure of men and women to express and be attuned to each other's feelings and thoughts.

There may be any number of reasons for this plight. If raised in an uncommunicative family, an individual may not have developed adequate verbal skills. Some people are shy; they may lack self-confidence: "Why should anyone want to listen to me? I have nothing important to say." Some are intimidated, while others are hostile and do not communicate in order not to antagonize. Still others are suspicious, self-protective, and, hence, secretive. Most often the deterioration of communication occurs gradually and is the result of an interactive process. John doesn't bring up issues for discussion because he finds Mary too critical of him. Mary is then critical of John's silence. John then concludes that he was right about Mary all along: she is a nag. Sometimes a partner will encourage communication and then discourage it by frequent interruptions, in effect, disqualifying the speaker and his or her message. Communication may also be impeded by confusing the spoken message with contradictory body language, speaking in an accusatory manner, lecturing, moralizing, and so on. Oftentimes, even the statement "we need to talk" takes on an emotional tone and is interpreted ominously: "Uh oh, he (she) wants to complain about me again."

While constrained communication results in relationship dissatisfaction, this is not to say that unbridled self-expression is synonymous with marital bliss. Indeed, there is a wealth of information to suggest that uncensored communication may be more than any relationship can bear. Such factors as timing, interest of the other person, appropriateness, and the effects of the disclosures on either party also must be considered. If a connection exists between self-expression and relationship satisfaction, research trends suggest it is curvilinear, not linear; that is, too much disclosure and too little disclosure may be associated with discord, while some intermediate amount, under appropriate conditions, is related to satisfaction.

More specifically, behavioral scientists have found that the impact of negative statements on people is greater than that of positive statements. "I really like you," in other words, is more than canceled out by "Drop dead." It may be that human beings are naturally and inherently more alert to negative cues. Being vigilant to negative and threatening cues in our environment may have proven adaptive (survival) value, and is possibly built into our psychological structure. Whatever the explanation, the effect of too much negativism is similar to the princess who was able to focus on the pea underneath the feather bed on which she lay: *The prevalence of negative expression, no matter how well intended or how eloquently expressed, draws attention away from positives and is likely to have a relationship-eroding effect.*

Is all this to say that honesty between a man and a woman had better be thrown to the wind? No, this is not the point. It is simply that blunt and "brutal" honesty seldom facilitates intimacy. Real intimacy does not mean full disclosure of one's thoughts, feelings, and actions. Real intimacy is experienced only when people have the capacity and wisdom to give and to withhold, to move toward and to move away from, to be close and to be distant. In the great majority of relationships, total openness and closeness are oppressive and smothering goals.

Although totally "free" disclosures—particularly when of an excessively negative nature—are not necessarily a blessing, as a general rule, most of us agree that knowing little of what our partner thinks, feels, and wants is distressing and quite unpleasant. Therefore, the objective of the Communication Principles that follow is to develop the listening, expressive, request-making, feedback, and clarifying skills needed to enhance a relationship.

THE EMPATHIC-LISTENING PRINCIPLE

The Empathic-Listening Principle: Effective listening involves a commitment to fully attend to the speaker's message, particularly the emotional component, and to relay this to the speaker in such a way that he or she feels accepted and understood.

It is easy to misread or overlook feelings. This indifference starts in childhood, when many of us learn to hide our feelings. Later, when we go to school, we learn about math, geography, and grammar, but feelings are rarely part of the curriculum. As adults, we are busy: we have goals to reach, achievements to attain; and days pass quickly without much attention to feelings. Your job may be shaky, one of your children may be sick, and you may have a cold coming on; but if a casual friend asks in passing how you feel, you will probably reply, "I'm fine." This kind of superficial exchange is merely a sign of friendliness, not an expression of feelings. Life is full of such rituals, of harmless small talk. The trouble is that over the years these shallow, habitual responses become so ingrained that we devalue the importance of our own feelings and those of the significant people in our lives.

A lifetime of inattentiveness to feelings is strikingly demonstrated by Martin, a musician, and Gloria, his wife of twenty years. Two months before this conversation, Gloria had discovered Martin's long-standing infidelity:

Martin: I don't think we've ever been a team intimately. I've never felt close to you. I've always felt you were my doll. You were my gracious hostess, my lovely lady, my bride. But I don't think I ever made total love to you. I loved you with reservation. As though you were a piece of art and would surely break if I were to release my passion on you and in you. So, throughout the years, I've sought to release this passion with other women . . . Gloria, how did you feel about the relationship all these years?

Gloria: How did I feel? Well . . . I suppose lonely. I wanted to be more passionate with you, less reserved; but I always felt you would reject me. I always felt you wanted me up on a pedestal. I stayed there to keep you.

Martin: (stunned) But, Gloria, I never knew that. Why didn't you tell me how you felt? Why didn't you say something?

Gloria: Afraid, I guess. You never asked. I thought that was the way you wanted things. Why didn't *you* ever say anything?

Martin: (crying) For the same reasons, I suppose. I took it for granted that you were happy with the status quo. I didn't want to hurt you or be hurt. God, I wish I had known how you felt back then, Gloria! I didn't really want to see other women. I wanted intimacy. Closeness. We could have given that to each other.

The waste of time, energy, and potential happiness through the years of Martin and Gloria's marriage, when what they both *really* wanted was so much more similar than what they each *supposed* the other wanted, is appalling. Yet this same kind of waste characterizes millions of relationships. A main cause is the failure of men and women to be attuned to each other's feelings. To understand thoroughly another person's thoughts and feelings and to be understood thoroughly by this other person in return are among the most rewarding of human experiences and, unfortunately, all too rare. In the examples that follow, we will see how a couple interact ineffectively and how the same issues can be discussed more sensitively.

Judy and Jerry have been married for eight years. They have two children, ages five and six. Jerry is an executive in a large electronics firm. He has a good job, and they live very comfortably. Jerry drives home from work on a summer evening and is greeted at the door by an exuberant Judy.

Judy: Hi, sweetheart. I've got great news.

Jerry: Terrific. What's up?

Judy: I could hardly wait until tonight to tell you. Remember how I've mentioned my boredom and feelings of uselessness in the past? Well, today I did something about them. I went over to the college, filled out an application form, and had an interview for the nursing program. I was told my chances for acceptance are very good, and it is likely I'll be starting in September. I'm so excited!

Jerry: (angrily) What about the kids? What about your responsibilities here? How the hell can you start school with all that? Nothing doing! We don't need extra expenses and more chaos!

Judy: (angrily and defensively) Who the hell do you think you are? You can't live my life for me. I'm bored, I want something meaningful to do, and I'm going back to school.

Jerry: Oh, no, you aren't!

Judy: Oh, yes, I am!

Jerry: I won't let you. I'm not going to give you the money.

Judy: That won't stop me. You bastard! I'll borrow the money. I'm tired of being bored, depressed, and burdened. No one's going to stop me from taking care of myself.

Jerry: Is that all you think you are, a housewife?

Judy: No, I'm much more. I'm a babysitter, cook, window washer, waxer, cleaner, and clerk—and I've had it. I start school next month, and that's all there is to it!

Jerry: You can't.

Judy: I can and I am. That's final.

Jerry: You're not and that's final.

Here's a replay of this couple's conversation, this time with each recognizing and respecting the other's feelings.

Judy: Hi, sweetheart. I've got great news.

Jerry: You really seem excited. What's up?

Judy: I am excited. I could hardly wait until tonight to tell you. Today I finally did something to counter the boredom and sense of uselessness I've been experiencing. I went over to the college, filled out the application form, and had an interview for the nursing program. I was told my chances for acceptance are very good, and it is likely I'll be starting in September.

Jerry: Gee, you really seem high about this. I wish I could share your enthusiasm about going back to school, but I have mixed feelings about it.

Judy: Mixed feelings? I don't understand. Why are your feelings mixed?

Jerry: I'm not sure. It's so sudden, I haven't had a chance to think about it . . . On the one hand, I'm glad you're enthused about something. I know you've been down in the dumps for a while. But there's something frightening to me about this. I also feel funny that something as important to you as going back to school wasn't discussed with me until now.

Judy: It sounds as if you are really thrown by this. It really is kind of sudden. I've been thinking about it for a few days, and when I decided to do it, I wanted to surprise you. It seems I shocked you instead.

Jerry: You did. That's for sure. There are lots of things that scare me about this.

Judy: For example?

Jerry: What about the kids? Are they going to be short-changed?

Judy: Well, both of them are going to be in school in the fall. I met with a counselor today and planned a tentative course schedule that doesn't conflict with their school hours.

I'll be able to make it home substantially before them in the afternoon.

Jerry: Boy, you've really planned this thing out. It must mean a great deal to you.

Judy: It does. It is vitally important to me. And so are you and the children. But I recognize that I have been restless and out of sorts for a long time now. I have been inattentive to myself and my own needs. I've been bored. There is no challenge in my life.

Jerry: You aren't satisfied with the loving feelings we all have for you?

Judy: I am, Jerry. But it isn't enough. We all have strong feelings for you. Would you be satisfied to stop work, stay home, and be a "housefather"?

Jerry: Come on now. You know that wouldn't be enough for me.

Judy: I feel the same way. It's not that these other things aren't important, but I miss the stimulation of the world outside this house.

Jerry: I have to say this, Judy, I'm also worried that you'll be less available to me when you start school.

Judy: It's true that I'll probably be busier and have less time for you, Jerry. But I'll have a renewed zest for life. I think this will be communicated to you and the children. I believe I can be a better person and, consequently, a better mother by not ignoring my own development.

Jerry: You present a pretty convincing case, Judy, but I can't say that I'm totally comfortable with the idea. I appreciate how important this venture is to you and I respect your right to pursue it. I realize that if I were in your place, I would do the same thing.

Judy: I understand this will be a transition for you as well as for me, Jerry, and there may be some difficulties that will have to be worked out. But I'm confident things will fall into place.

In this couple's first conversation, they quickly became adversaries. Their dialogue was primarily authoritarian and judgmental ("We don't need extra expenses and more chaos!"); threatening and counterthreatening (I'm not going to give you the money"; "No one's going to stop me . . ."). This kind of dialogue rarely produces a resolution of the issue at hand, and both parties are likely to storm off bitter and resentful. The all-too-familiar result of this kind of exchange —which may be yelled, signaled by angry glances, or telegraphed by hurt silence—is: "Everything would have worked out fine if you hadn't upset me" or "You just don't give a damn about my feelings." Building trust and resolving important personal issues satisfactorily require recognition of and respect for a partner's feelings and point of view. These qualities were conspicuously lacking in the first dialogue.

In the replay dialogue, although Judy and Jerry were not in total agreement about the issue (". . . I can't say that I'm comfortable with the idea"), they communicated an understanding of each other's position and feelings ("It must mean a great deal to you" and "This will be a transition for you as well as for me, Jerry"). It was as if they were silently asking, "How does he (she) see it? How does he (she) feel? How would I feel if this were said to me?" This is empathy, a critical ingredient in mutually satisfying relationships. It is an effort to understand another's beliefs, practices, and feelings without necessarily sharing or agreeing with them. While empathy does not require agreement with the other's view, it does preclude the demand that "You must think, feel, and act like me." Empathic relating is actually a radical departure from usual forms of relating. Many of us are unaware of the tremendous pressure we put on our family members to have the same feelings we do. It is often as though we silently say, "If you want me to love you, then you must have the same feelings I do. If I feel your behavior is bad, you must feel so too. If I feel a certain goal is desirable, you must feel so too."

Corrective Prescription

Empathy is made up of two main components. One is listening and attempting to understand another's view rather than busily preparing a rebuttal; the second is communicating this understanding to the speaker. A small exercise that frequently helps to develop this pattern of communicating is role reversal. In this exercise, when a discussion involving differences of personal/emotional issues occurs, it becomes the responsibility of each party to state the partner's position and feelings until he is satisfied with the degree of understanding achieved. If he is not satisfied, a brief "time-out" is called while his position and related feelings are expressed again. The discussion does not proceed until each partner is satisfied that the salient aspects of his position are understood. For example:

Him: I'm out there all day long, getting one turndown after another. Being a salesman is tough. Some days it really gets to me.

Her: Cooking and cleaning—that's my day. What the hell are you complaining about?

Him: Hold it. Time out! You passed right over my feelings. Can you please restate what I said from *my* viewpoint? [He is asking for an empathic response.]

Her: It sounded as if you were trying to make me feel guilty, and I won't have any of that. [Rather than looking at his feelings she is still focusing on her own.]

Him: That wasn't my intention. I was just feeling a bit frustrated. Do you understand? [He is restating his position and asking her to express *his* position in her own words.]

Her: I understand now. You are feeling frustrated after a day of rejection. It's just that I had a lousy day, also.

Him: Sounds like you are also pretty frustrated. What's the matter? . . .

If a man and woman conscientiously perform this exercise, though it may seem forced and silly at the beginning, many difficulties not caused by actual differences but by the misunderstanding and emotional alienation will be prevented. What's more, when feelings are identified and expressed in an empathic manner, a couple will sometimes find that the real difficulty has little to do with what they are arguing about. An argument about flirting at social gatherings, for instance, might be only a symptom of two people's assumptions: "If you loved me, you wouldn't do this" or "If you respected me, you'd trust me." The fears behind the assumption are quite similar: "I'm afraid you don't love/respect me." At this level, seeming differences turn into shared experiences; that is, each partner might feel emotionally threatened by the flirting or the command to stop, and the surface disagreement may be only an expression of the differences in the way each partner avoids or copes with very similar feelings and experiences. Only by being sensitive to each other's feelings will a couple achieve a level of discussion where these discoveries occur.

Because it is when emotions are strongest that it is most difficult to achieve empathic communication, a third party, such as a close friend who is able to lay aside his or her own feelings and evaluations, can assist greatly by listening with understanding to each person and clarifying the views and attitudes each holds. When the individuals in the dispute realize they are being understood, that someone sees how the situation seems to them, the statements are likely to grow less exaggerated and defensive, and it is no longer necessary to maintain the attitude "I am one hundred percent right and you are one hundred percent wrong." Along with decreased defensiveness comes a clarification of the issues, which opens the path toward resolution. Obviously, though, if the issue is never explored in depth, if superficiality is maintained by mutual recrimination and insult, the likelihood of successful resolution is minimal.

THE "I MESSAGE" PRINCIPLE

The "I Message" Principle: It is important to take clear responsibility for every message you send, whether in the form of a statement or in the form of a question, for that is the only way to enter into personal dialogue.

In striking contrast to the enthusiasm of courtship, conversation in many post-honeymoon relationships becomes painfully strained:

She: You never talk to me.

He: What's on your mind?

She: It's not what's on my mind; it's that I never know what's on your mind.

He: What do you want to know?

She: Everything!

He: That's ridiculous.

She: (angrily) I'll bet you don't think talking to that blond assistant of yours is ridiculous.

He: Aw, come on, cut it out.

She: (on the verge of tears) You never want to talk to me anymore the way you did when we first met.

He: Here we go again.

In its most comprehensive definition, "to communicate" means "to make known"; to give to another; to exchange thoughts, feelings, and information; to share; to develop a connecting link. Connecting on an intimate basis requires that both people in a relationship reveal themselves in a personal manner.

An important step in this direction is to make ourselves known through personalizing our conversations. Too often, though, as psychiatrist Walter Kempler reports in *Principles of Gestalt Family Therapy*, an opposite process occurs. Held back by fear and influenced by conventional social discourse, we use language that masks our personal reactions. For instance, we refer to important events in remote "it" language:

She: I feel very much alone, separate from you. I don't like my feeling.
He: What should we do about it?

In the man's response to this woman's statement, the feeling has become an impersonal "it" and the tense has been changed to the future. The risk now is that the conversation will move too quickly to planning future ways of correcting the situation without exploring the feeling involved. A more personal response to her pain, which includes a measure of immediacy, would be simply, "How do I contribute to your aloneness?"

Using "it" is often appropriate in business situations. Indeed, most places of employment reward the worker for his or her ability to focus exclusively on "it": the product to be sold, the work to be done. Personal reaction is restricted to the suggestion box, a co-worker, or perhaps aired in a special brainstorming or gripe meeting under controlled guidance.

In marked contrast, personal conversation emphasizes what is going on inside a person, since the object is to become known. Here, elements that are quite commonplace in professional or casual conversation are either unnecessary or potentially damaging. In this regard, statements beginning with "it" externalize responsibility; the listener finds it difficult to respond because the speaker has not accepted ownership of what he or she has said. For instance, in the statement "It is difficult talking to you," "it" is out there somewhere, part of neither the speaker nor the listener. A sentence that communicates more intimately is "I have difficulty talking to you."

"It" statements are under-responsible because they leave ownership of the feeling or thought in question; "we," "everybody," and "all" statements are over-responsible because they pass ownership to everyone (and therefore to no one in particular), and so tend to diffuse experience: "*Most* people would be angry about this"; "There are *those* who believe in capital punishment"; "*Everybody* else liked the movie"; "*We* need to budget more conservatively." In these statements, neither party feels or thinks something; it is the nebulous "we" or "them" that is being referred to; and responsibility is diluted. "We need to budget more conservatively" may be restated with ownership as "I am concerned about our finances and I want you to spend less money." In addition to whitewashing a personal reaction, over-responsible statements are often used to provoke an individual to feel guilty or incompetent. The disguised intent of "everybody else liked the movie," for example, might be "Since you are in the minority, there must be something wrong with you."

While "we" and "it" statements dilute responsibility, sentences that begin with "you" are almost always accusatory and engender feelings of defensiveness on the part of the listener; "you" statements, on the other hand, involve an effort to shift responsibility for a reaction from the speaker to the listener. Contrast the following statements:

You don't love me.	I wish I could feel loved by you.
You make me nervous.	I am afraid.
You make me mad.	I am angry at you.
You are too bossy.	I hate when you tell me what to do.

"You" statements are actually "I" statements in disguise. If an individual is upset, it is easy for him to avoid responsibility by indicating "It's your fault!" "You" statements are essential to the blaming game. When sentences begin with "you," the speaker's part in any difference or dissension is omitted. When the sentence begins with "I," there is an acknowledgment of personal responsibility; it is harder to put all the blame on the listener.

Just as most statements like "You make me mad" are actually personal statements saying "I feel angry," so are most questions camouflaged statements. The purpose of questions is to obtain information, but questions also direct attention to the other person and tend to put him or her on the defensive. "Do you have another woman?" risks a defensive answer and futile argument. "There's something missing in our relationship, and I would like to talk about it" is the question converted into a statement. The statement emphasizes the speaker's responsibility for his or her position rather than allowing it to remain hidden behind the question.

Questions often veer conversations off course. A woman repeatedly asks her partner, "What do you think of me?" Her partner tries various answers, generally reassuring, but to no avail. When the woman converts her question into a statement, personal conversation is propelled forward:

She: I want you to think well of me, to assure me that I am a good wife. I live in constant fear that I am not.

He: I did not know how you felt. I love and respect you. Perhaps I need to express my affection differently.

As with "you" statements, questions are often accusations. A man asks his partner, "Where did you go? Who were you with?"; "Why are you driving so fast?"; "Why are you wearing that blouse?" When unscrambled, these are all subtle forms of criticism. This is particularly the case if the question begins with "why": "Why shouldn't I think of myself?"; "Why must you worry so much?"; "Why can't you remember my messages?"; "Why are you so uptight?"; "Why are you wearing that jacket?"

Each of these questions is a thinly concealed criticism that reinforces the speaker in a "one-up" position, holding the listener "one-down." Each is unaswerable because it implies the listener has done something wrong and demands that he or she justify or alter his or her behavior. Rather than increasing understanding, most "why" questions begin an endless exchange of rationalizations and explanations that move a couple further and further from intimacy.

Sometimes questions are traps that spring once the respondent has committed him or herself. "When did you get home?" asks a man in an apparently innocent request for information. But if the man already knows that his partner came home late and is angry she didn't call, then the question is not so innocent; it is a deceitful, vague expression of a feeling: "I know you came home late last night and I'm angry that you didn't call to inform me"; or, "I want you to show me that you care by calling and I'm hurt that you didn't." As it stood, the intent of the question was manipulative. If the response is honest, it gives the angry man "permission" to show his anger; and if the response is a lie, it offers him the opportunity to begin a game of "I gotcha."

Still another means of diluting responsibility for our thoughts and feelings comes in the form of qualifiers and disclaimers: "If you don't mind me saying so . . ."; "I might be wrong, but . . ."; "I know you're sensitive, however . . ."; "This might sound silly, but . . ."; "Although you probably disagree. . . ." The disclaimer can also be a phrase tacked on after a slightly challenging remark: "It was an awful evening —wasn't it?"; "We should rearrange our priorities—I think"; "I'll go along with your judgment—I guess." Each disclaimer apologizes for the speaker's temerity in daring to offer an opinion. The disclaimer also gives the listener "permission" to disagree.

Stripping away qualifiers and disclaimers brings force and vitality back into a statement; contrary to most formal education, which urges a modesty many of us do not possess, qualifiers obscure and drain the personal element from a conversation.

Corrective Prescription

Self-expressive statements provide your partner with a personalized message that enables him or her to know you more intimately. In addition, an individual can make better sense of his or her own inner experience by translating that experience into words.

The most important step in personalizing conversations is to begin statements with a form of the pronoun "I" ("Me," "my," "mine"). "I" statements, as psychologist Thomas Gordon suggests in *Parent Effectiveness Training*, are expressions of responsibility; beginning a sentence with "I" leaves no question as to the ownership of an opinion or reaction. Speaking for oneself in this manner establishes the speaker as the sole authority on his awareness; and it declares that the speaker's thoughts, feelings, and intentions have importance. Note that tacking a prefix like "I think that you . . ." or "I feel that you . . ." onto a sentence does not make it an "I" statement. An "I" statement is a report of an individual's awareness of himself, not of the other person: "I wish I felt loved by you" rather than "I feel that you don't love me."

To further increase the benefits of self-statements, it is important that they be present-oriented. This requires limiting your personal observations to the present tense. ("That bothers me" rather than "That could be disturbing") and to immediate experience ("I see you staring into space and not responding to my questions" rather than "You never pay attention to me").

Questions, as we have seen, can also mask personal reactions. Certainly not all questions are illegitimate, manipulative devices; in fact, there are two specific circumstances in which questions can be very useful in personal conversations: (1) when feedback is wanted ("What's your reaction?"); and (2) for clarification ("I'm not sure I understand. Do you mean . . . ?").

In the interest of taking responsibility for your own position or preference, before asking a question of an intimate, attempt to convert it into a statement. When questions are asked, they should be preceded by a self-statement. For example, Julie might ask Walter if he has plans for Saturday afternoon. A yes from Walter may provoke an outburst from Julie in which she accuses him of always making plans without her. On the other hand, a no is likely to be accompanied by an apprehension on Walter's part that he is about to commit himself before he knows to what. In contrast, if Julie were to take responsibility for her message first (*i.e.*, "I am going shopping tomorrow afternoon") and then ask her question (*i.e.*, "Would you like to come with me?"), Walter would not feel as if he had been set up.

It is preferable to use "how" and "what" rather than the accusatorial "why" to begin questions. "How" and "what" contribute to a problem-solving orientation: "What is the matter?" can lead to a clarification of an issue, while "why are you feeling bad?" often lends itself to lengthy and unnecessary justification for feeling bad.

To enhance the positive tone of a question, it is often useful to follow up with a second question that draws on the answer to the first. Compare the following two exchanges:

He: How were sales today?
She: Pretty slow. I wasn't really able to get rolling today.
He: Sales in my company have really improved, as a matter of fact . . .

It is clear from this exchange that the question was not so much an expression of interest as a prop for the questioner's speech. In contrast:

He: How are sales today?
She: Pretty slow. I had one of those, sorry-I-got-up-this-morning days.
He: Are you upset about your progress?

Clearly, in this exchange, the second question can be taken as an expression of genuine interest.

In sum, *statements should begin with "I," and be declarative, present-oriented*, and *free of qualifiers and disclaimers*. When questions are asked, it is preferable that they be (1) *preceded by a statement*, (2) *emphasize "how" and "what,"* and (3) *be followed by a second question*.

Herewith follows a series of brief exercises that can heighten awareness of self-expressive statements.

1.   Talk to your partner about any aspect of the relationship for about five minutes. The only restriction on the conversation is that each sentence begin with "it."

Now briefly discuss the experience of making only "it" statements. How do you feel sending and receiving these types of statements?

2. Repeat the exercise above, this time using only "you" statements. Then, again, using "we" statements.

Now talk to each other, beginning each sentence with "I." No statements are permitted that do not begin with "I." Each statement should make direct reference to your partner. For instance, "I appreciate your loyalty" or "I don't like being rejected by you."

Compare this experience with your previous "it," "you," and "we" conversations. Be particularly aware of which types of statements improve clarity and the listener's receptivity to the speaker.

3. In this exercise, each partner is to ask a "why" question ("Why are you going out tonight?") and immediately convert the question into an "I" statement ("I would like you home with me tonight"). Take turns doing this for about five minutes.

Discuss your experience during this exchange. How did you feel as the sender and receiver of the questions? Compare your reaction to being the sender and receiver of "I" statements.

Learning the "I Message" Principle is likely to be hastened

by applying it to everyday situations. This can be accomplished by being aware of the types of statements you or others make in conversations. Silently convert the "it," "you," or "we" statements, as well as the questions of others, into "I" statements. Notice how each type of statement affects what is being discussed, and how you feel as sender and receiver of each type of statement.

THE DIRECT-COMMUNICATION PRINCIPLE

The Direct-Communication Principle: When something is wanted—be it change, clarification, reassurance, companionship, or support—it is important that the message sent be direct and to the point. Speaking in generalities and expecting the listener to "mind read" won't get the job done.

Communication in relationships is a constant. When a man and a woman can hear or observe each other, there is the potential for an exchange of information. Messages are sent verbally or through body or facial expressions. The words of the message may relate straightforward and factual information—"I want to eat" or "I put gas in the car" or "It is cold" —or the tone of voice or gesture may indicate another level of interpretation of the message is necessary. Sometimes the meaning of a message is hard to decipher. This is particularly true when indirectness and subtlety play a major role in a relationship. When messages are not straightforward, couples typically assume that they understand what their partners mean by certain actions, feel in certain situations, or intend by various words or gestures or tone of voice. Frequently they are wrong. Acting on the erroneous assumption, however, will often trigger a partner to respond negatively, thus reaffirming and further entrenching the "mind reader's" position that he was "right in the first place."

Janet and Dan have been married three years. They were both married before. When Dan was still married to his first wife, he had an affair with Janet, who was divorced. Although Dan and Janet were both affected by their brief encounter (it happened during one of Dan's business trips), it was not pursued at the time because of Dan's marriage. Two months later, Dan's wife left him for another man. Six months after that, Dan and Janet were married. Because he slept with her while he was still married to his first wife, Janet worries that Dan will have affairs while married to her. She is secretly suspicious of him. Dan regards his infidelity in his previous marriage an exception to his usual behavior, and views the motivation behind it as desperation. His marriage had been deteriorating for a long time, and he acted quite out of his character. He operates from a standpoint of fidelity and trust with Janet. She, in turn, is guided by mistrust and her suspicious attitude: "If he did it to his previous wife, he will probably do it to me." Consequently, their discussions about absences from home, particularly business trips, are filled with misunderstanding:

Janet: You know what, I think I'll go to Chicago with you, Dan. Maybe I can be of some help to you there.

Dan: That's okay, Jan. I'm provided with a nice hotel room, meals, transportation, and so on. I don't really need any help.

Janet: (disappointed) Oh, then I can keep you company.

Dan: (starting to experience a vague sense of guilt) Jan, it's nice of you to want to be with me, but my schedule keeps me busy from nine in the morning to midnight; and since it wouldn't be appropriate for you to sit in on business meetings, I would hardly see you.

Janet: (persistent with a trace of annoyance in her voice) I think I'd like to go anyway.

Dan: (with impatience and annoyance) Listen, the company won't pay your way, and I would hardly see you, so there's no point in our spending an extra five hundred dollars that we can ill afford for nothing. Let's leave it at that.

Janet: Let's not leave it at that. I'm going!

Dan: (angrily and with frustration) Shit! Janet, for Christ's sake, when you get so damned unreasonable, I feel as if I don't know you anymore. You're not like the woman I married.

Janet: (her anxiety and resentment escalating) That's it! You don't want to be with me anymore. I knew it! You're looking for someone else . . .

Conversations based on indirectness and private, untested assumptions such as Janet's and Dan's are frequently disastrous. In this instance, Dan assumes Janet is merely being pigheaded. Janet, of course, assumes Dan, cornered, is purposely evasive. Had she directly stated her concern or had Dan asked why the trip was so important, the outcome might have been different. It is probable that these patterns of behavior are somewhat present in almost all relationships: there is an argument whose source is unclear or camouflaged; the result after many futile bouts is often of the you-hurt-me-so-I'll-hurt-you variety; and, in many instances, vindicativeness becomes the major force in the gradual weakening of the relationship.

As the negativity created by indirectness escalates, it spills over into other areas of the relationship; that is, once a negative, destructive atmosphere of misunderstanding has been established, more indirectness and misunderstanding are likely to follow as protection against the "enemy." For example, Janet may begin to attack Dan on any number of insignificant issues: his dress, his manners, his parenting, and so on. In actuality, Janet's criticisms are related to something entirely different: she is insecure and afraid of losing Dan. Stating her real concern in the attack-counterattack atmosphere of her own making, however, would leave her feeling vulnerable. Instead, she is caught in a series of relationship-defeating attempts to allay her anxiety while avoiding a straightforward discussion of her concern.

In marriage therapy, as Dr. Paul Watzlawick and his associates describe in their book *Change*, one frequently sees both spouses caught in a futile push-pull based on indirectly expressed speculations. For instance, a wife may have the impression that her husband is not open enough for her to know where she stands with him, what is going on in his head, what he is doing when he is away from home, and so on. Quite naturally, she will therefore attempt to make herself more secure by asking him questions, watching his behavior, and checking on him in a variety of other ways. He is likely to consider her behavior intrusive and react by withholding from her information that in and of itself would be quite harmless and irrelevant, "just to teach her that I am not a child in need of checking." Rather than making her back down, her husband's reaction increases her insecurity and provides further fuel for her worries and her distrust: "If he does not talk to me about even these little things, he *must* be hiding something." The less information he gives her, the more persistently will she seek it; and the more she seeks it, the less he will give her. It is not long before the drama evolves to a point that Dr. Watzlawick views as reminiscent of two sailors hanging out of either side of a sailboat in order to steady it: the more the one leans overboard, the more the other has to hang out to compensate for the instability created by the other's attempts at stabilizing the boat, while the boat itself would be quite steady if not for the insecurities of its passengers. It is predictable that unless something changes in this situation—the couple discuss their assumptions openly and explicitly—the occupants of the boat—marriage—will be under constant unnecessary strain or, worse yet, finish up in the water. A direct and pointed statement by one of the partners may not, in fact, *resolve* a relationship issue. It may result in an admission that indeed there is a problem. The essential factor is that a clear exchange—where the message sent is the message received—provides the means for discussion. The couple may even conclude that they are at a temporary impasse; that is, they may agree that they disagree on some issue. This recognition, although it may seem limited, is a start. It is preferable to the undercurrent of torment and nagging uncertainty that accompanies obfuscation.

Yet another variation of indirectness that fosters ill will and confusion is the disguised request. A couple has just come out of the water after a delightful moonlit swim. The woman says, "Let's go inside. I'm sleepy." The man responds, "It's nice out here. Why don't we lie and rest here?" The woman, angry, storms into the house. The man, equally angry, drives off to a local bar. What has happened? She, by saying she was "sleepy," was actually signaling her desire to make love in the house. He, ironically, was signaling his desire to make love in the moonlight. Neither directly said what he or she wanted, and both felt rejected by the other. The evening ended in anger and hurt rather than in pleasure. Preventing this unfortunate turn of events may have been as simple as saying, "Let's go inside. I'm in the mood to make love" or "It's nice out here. Why don't we make love in the moonlight?"

Many requests are not expressed openly and directly. Often we don't want to take responsibility for our requests, so we hide and disguise them in questions, hints, obscure suggestions, and countless other manipulations, all in an effort to satisfy our desires without the risk of being rejected.

Open requests require an awareness of our desires and involve several risks: (1) an acknowledgment that the other person has something to offer that is of value. This recognition poses a particular threat to couples engaged in a power struggle. By asking for less or asking in a disguised form, the asker "discounts" the spouse's power; (2) being asked to reciprocate. Doubting one's willingness or capacity to satisfy the other's requests, one may prefer to stay self-contained rather than being reciprocal; (3) rejection. Many of us have a fear of the word "no"; and, by being vague, we hope to temper the pain of refusal.

The problem with requests, as with all indirect messages, is that those that are not understood are less likely to be satisfied. What's more, resentment often accompanies the unmet desire and is expressed in disguised form through nagging, criticism, and other kinds of annoyances and frustrations. Ultimately, the opportunity for a compromise, or at least some understanding of the refusal, is lost.

Corrective Prescription

There is no guaranteed way to avoid misunderstanding with a partner, but one thing is sure: coaxing, cajoling, dropping "cute" hints, manipulating, and beating around the bush are all barriers to clear communication. "Did you pick up the groceries today?" Alice asks John. Since John has arrived home without the groceries, Alice's question didn't have to be asked. What she was saying was "Why are you so late? I wish you had picked up the groceries." Or John may say to Alice, after they spent the evening at the home of friends, "Mary certainly comes up with unusual meals, doesn't she?" What John is really conveying by his tone of voice, though, is more like, "Why don't you cook more interesting dishes?"

When something is wanted—be it change, clarification, reassurance, companionship, or support—it is important that the message be direct and to the point. Speaking in generalities will not get the message across.

Here are some exercises to help focus your awareness on unexpressed and oblique communication. Each is designed to be completed while you and your partner are sitting face to face. It is very important to maintain eye contact throughout. Making some kind of physical contact as well is likely to deepen the involvement and increase the probability of learning something about your partner, yourself, and how you interact.

1. For about five minutes, alternate saying sentences to each other that begin with the words "I assume." Fill in the sentence with assumptions about your partner (e.g., "I assume you hate visiting my parents"); yourself ("I assume you know how critically important a promotion is to me"); or the relationship ("I assume you are pleased with our sexual experiences").

Don't discuss the assumptions; simply alternate making statements beginning with "I assume." If you get stuck, stay with it. Repeat the beginning of the sentence and see what words come to you.

After five minutes or so, discuss what each of you experienced and check out your assumptions. What did you discover about your own and your partner's assumptions? To what extent were your assumptions refuted? Which of those are you willing to revise? Take at least half an hour to discuss these issues with your partner.

2. In this exercise, each partner is to alternate making requests. Taking turns, begin each sentence with "I want you to." Be very specific about your request. Avoid generalities such as "I want you to please me." State in detail *how* and *when* you would like to be pleased. For example, "I want you to kiss me when I come home from work." The listening partner is not to reply to these requests. Take turns expressing requests for a total of five minutes.

Now take another few minutes each and summarize your understanding of your partner's requests. Clear up any misunderstanding but do not express agreement or disagreement with a particular request. The emphasis here is on understanding, on assuring your partner that the message sent is the message received.

When mutual understanding has been established, discuss

your feelings about each other's requests. Which of your own requests are really important to you? Which of your partner's requests are you desirous of meeting and which are you reluctant or unwilling to meet?

In what manner do you normally make requests of one another: Are they straightforward or indirect, such as "You don't want to go to the store for me, do you? If only I had time to get there myself." "Are you expecting to be busy all day today?" What's the basis for your disguised requests? Take at least a half hour to discuss these issues with your partner.

Follow up this exercise with an actual request. Note the wording being suggested for making requests: (1) begin with "I"; (2) be specific; and (3) use "want" (desire, prefer, like) rather than "need." A want is something that is desired but not necessary. "Need" implies that something is critical to survival, which is hardly ever the case in request making.

In addition to the appropriate phrasing for the request, consider the timing. Try to select a time when the probability of success is high. Do not make a request when your partner is obviously busy, tired, or otherwise out-of-sorts. If your partner's cues as to availability are ambiguous, ask for clarification.

3. In this last exercise, one partner is to request something that his or her partner is *unwilling* to grant. Make this request repeatedly. With each repetition, the unwilling partner is to say no without actually saying no (e.g.," I'll think about it"; "Let's discuss it later"). Be aware of the nature of the evasions.

Continue for about four minutes, switch places, and resume for another four minutes. After both partners have had a turn being the requester and the evader, discuss the experience: What did you learn about your own and your partner's ways of avoiding a direct no?

At the same time that no is acceptable, requests may also be seen as negotiable. Carl is asked by Phyllis to paint their bedroom. Carl assumes that the job will consume his entire day off. Rather than saying no, he suggests that if Phyllis will buy the equipment and prepare the room for painting, he will do it. In that way, he reasons, he can complete the job in a few hours and have time for his own recreation.

THE PRINCIPLE OF WEAK WORDS AND STRONG GESTURES

The Principle of Weak Words and Strong Gestures: Whenever our verbal and nonverbal forms of communication are discrepant—when our words convey one message but our tone of voice or body another—we are likely to arouse suspicion and confusion in the listener.

In the drama of human communication, the nonverbal dimension is critically important. Research indicates that about 70 percent of our communication with others is carried out on a nonverbal level. Analysis of slow-motion films of couples in various situations reveals that the two individuals continually "speak" to each other in nonverbal modes (gestures, actions, facial expressions, and the like). When a couple are in discord, for example, messages abound without their uttering a word. Strategic avoidance of eye contact, the utilization of eye rolling and expressions of disgust, the tendency to glare at one's partner, clenched hands, quick movements, all of these are powerful indications of negativity.

The most profound form of nonverbal communication is, of course, sex. But the ways in which your mate walks, stands, holds his or her head, makes (or avoids) eye contact, smiles, or frowns are also important; often these cues tell you far more than words.

Behavioral scientists have found that most of us rely on

nonverbal behavior as a means of communicating attraction or disdain in a social encounter. The face, followed by the hands and the feet, are considered sources of the most fertile cues to the meaning of a communication. For example, if a husband suggests sex to his wife and she says no, the meaning of her response can be clarified by the facial expression that accompanies it. If, as she says no, she smiles, she may be signaling: "Don't just ask, seduce me, be playful." If she frowns and presses her lips together angrily, her refusal is scornful and decisive: "I'm angry. How can you expect me to be intimate after embarrassing me last night!" If she offers a meek no, exhaling emphatically, as she responds, her decline may be more delay than refusal: "I'm pretty tired now, but perhaps later—or tomorrow." In each instance, the same verbal response was given, but the unspoken accompaniment relayed a very different message.

In the same vein, if a woman asks a man his feelings about her, his response of "I love you" would be greatly strengthened if he maintained eye contact while speaking. Moving his open hands toward her would say something very different than clenching his fists when he answers. And sitting with his knees tightly closed together would express a very different feeling than would his answering her question while reaching toward her with open, outstretched legs.

Related to the nonverbal aspect of a communication is the style of delivery. The Fasts, in *Talking Between the Lines*, focus their sharp gaze on the tone, rhythm, and volume of voice, as well as the emotional overlay we give to words; sarcasm, tenderness, irritability.

Consider the simple factual statement "I cleared the kitchen table." A partner may say this in a haughty tone of voice that conveys "I'm so much better than you, you're such a slob," or a friendly tone that says, "I'm glad to be able to help out." An intimate may request help cleaning the table in a heavy voice that says, "I'm exhausted, please lend a hand"; a hurt tone that says, "Poor me, you always leave me the dirty work"; or an angry tone that says, "Damn you, I resent having to remind you about cleaning up."

The rhythm of a message—where the emphasis is placed and the pacing—adds another dimension. Even Muriel, a three-year-old child, is sensitive to these undercurrents. Muriel's parents consider themselves civilized; they never fight in front of Muriel. "In fact," they boast, "we rarely even raise our voices in front of her." Yet Muriel senses that Mom and Dad are frequently angry.

"Don't be mad!" she pleads defensively when she tears her new dress. "Dad's not mad, honey. Mom should have saved the dress for a special occasion." Turning to his wife, he says, "I'm sure you can sew the tear, dear."

It seems a simple, even a loving request. The word "dear" is even thrown in. But Muriel hears nothing simple or loving in the statement. She hears the tight anger in her father's voice, his emphasis on "you," the slight but strategic pause before "dear."

On the surface Muriel's parents are communicating that everything is fine; this is a loving, cooperative family. But the manner of speaking, the music of the words, indicate that everything is not fine. Muriel is sensitized to these continual contradictions, and she reacts by developing an apologetic posture in an attempt to relieve her own anxiety and assuage the controlled rage between her parents.

Just as tone, rhythm, and accompanying emotion affect the meaning of a communication, volume also discloses a tremendous amount about an interaction. For example, a person of high status may raise his voice to someone of lower status; an officer may yell at an enlisted man, an executive at an underling, a teacher at a student, a parent at a child, a husband at a wife, a wife at a husband, depending on who is feeling superior at a particular time.

In contrast, volume often drops off, perhaps even to a whisper, under certain circumstances. A lowered voice may communicate caring, as when we comfort the bereaved; intimacy, by signaling, "What I have to say is for your ears alone"; the quiet before the storm, when the lowered volume is accomplished by slow, painstakingly deliberate speech through clenched teeth; or fear through "Don't attack me. I am lowering my voice to demonstrate my defenselessness."

Of course, as with other stylistic and nonverbal aspects of communication, meaning may vary depending on culture and background. In one family soft, melodic speech with only minor animation is associated with calm, loving messages. In another family, the voice and energy level are higher. Family members yell continually, orchestrating their speech with flailing arms. In this family, these are the signals of love and warmth.

In many cases, we simply become so used to our partner's nonverbal and stylistic signs that they cease to affect us on a conscious level. Sometimes, too, we deliberately screen them out or disregard them, either from impatience or misunderstood intent. Consider the following exchange:

The scene takes place around midnight at a house party. Gail is tired and eager to return home; her six-year-old has been ill, and she was up several times the previous night comforting him. Gail's husband, David, is seated next to Gloria, a young, attractive woman, and is heavily engrossed in conversation. Gail positions herself so that she is able to make eye contact with David and then taps her foot impatiently while motioning toward the door with her head.

David: (to himself) She's jealous; she wants me to leave.

Gloria: (to herself) His wife wants him to leave. Let's see what kind of choice he makes.

With this unspoken challenge, Gloria leans toward David and tosses her head back, letting her hair fall freely in a provocative manner.

David: (turns his back to his wife and thinks to himself) She's not going to order me around.

Gail: (to herself) What a selfish bastard! He knows I'm tired. Wait until we get home!

Gail and David's spat illustrates the importance of being sensitive to your partner's silent signals. In a very brief, wordless exchange, a plea to leave was sent and misunderstood; feelings of jealousy were interpreted; a challenge was offered by Gloria; and David reacted as if his "manhood" were at stake. Feelings of anger, seduction, hurt, and confusion ensued.

On other occasions, it is not so much that couples misread the nonverbal cues as that the nonverbal aspect of the message contradicts the spoken word. Larry may say to his wife, "I'm listening, I'm listening," while glancing at the morning newspaper. Allen may tell his wife, "I love you," over and over but say it in a flippant manner while focusing his attention elsewhere. The partners of both Allen and Larry have good cause to wonder about the reliability of the messages they are receiving.

Whenever our verbal and nonverbal forms of communication are discrepant—when our words convey one message but our tone of voice or body another—we are likely to arouse suspicion and confusion in the listener. Sometimes the discrepancy is a signal that there is an underlying problem in the relationship. Discovering the contradictions and discussing them may well bring to awareness unrecognized feelings, gripes, and desires. Larry was obviously more interested in the morning's news than in conversing with his wife. Larry could have said, "Couldn't we wait till later, Rita?" If Rita felt strongly about talking, she could have made this known. If she didn't, she could have respected Larry's desire to delay the conversation.

Larry and Rita were being overly polite in an attempt to create an impression that is unreasonable: We are *always* desirous of contact with each other. In actuality, both Larry and Rita were collecting "resentment stamps" in regard to this issue. Many couples are burdened with this and similar relationship-eroding demands. Most often, these demands are evident in nonverbal behavior. Recognizing and countering the irrational premises in a relationship can be aided immensely by paying attention to *how* a message is conveyed as well as to the content of the message. This is not to suggest that intimates should immediately clobber each other with "Aha, I caught you in a lie." Instead, a frank, nonaccusatory discussion of the contradiction can be used to lead to greater openness and trust in the relationship.

Corrective Prescription

The following are awareness-building exercises designed to alert couples to their stylistic and nonverbal signals. The intent is to develop consistency between *what* is said and *how* it is said.

1. Both partners are to sit together with eyes closed throughout. (Eliminating vision forces a heightened auditory sensitivity.) Initiate a discussion of importance to the relationship. You may discuss division of marital/parental responsibilities, in-laws, feelings about a recent issue, or any other topic of mutual interest.

As you do this focus your attention on your own and your partner's voices. See if you can listen as if the other person were speaking an unfamiliar language. Try to understand the message by listening to the emphasis, tone, rhythm, etc. Do this for about fifteen minutes.

Now discuss what you noticed about your own voice and your partner's. Be very specific in your commentary. What is the voice like? Is it strong or weak, clear or unclear, harsh or mellow? Is it judging, complaining, angry, pleading, hurt? Does the style fit the content? What effect does the voice and its stylistic variation have on you?

2. In this experience the goal is to highlight inconsistencies

in what the message receiver *hears* and what he or she *sees* expressed through body language.

Each spouse will alternate expressing a sentiment and canceling its meaning with a gesture, grimace, motion, facial expression, or some other nonverbal behavior. The sentiments, expressed in your own words, should include: (1) an expression of approval. (For example, as Jill compliments Mark on a decision he has made, she looks down, shakes her head side to side and plants her hands on her hips: all actions that signal disapproval and resignation to Mark); (2) a caring expression; and (3) an expression of availability (to problem solve, help with chores, do a favor, honor a request).

Be aware of how you feel as you send and receive these inconsistent communications. Discuss exactly what you and your partner do to cancel the verbal messages. Do any of these ways of canceling feel familiar?

After completing the discussion, change the body language and express approval, caring, and availability again. This time match the spoken word with the unspoken signals. Discuss the difference.

On a daily basis be alert to the unspoken cues of your spouse that express approval, caring, and availability.

3. Take turns repeating these three negative expressions, observing yourself (in a full-length mirror) and each other as you do so: "Right now I don't like you"; "You're being unreasonable and I won't continue listening"; "I suspect that you're lying."

Make each statement loudly, forcefully. At the same time be aware of how you are standing, what your body posture is like, how you hold your head, and so on. An intimate may offer a suggestion to be incorporated into the expression. Jane, observing Mitch, might say, "Look past me when you say, 'I don't like you.' That's what usually happens when you're mad." Demonstrate, if necessary.

After each partner has had an opportunity to act out the negative emotions associated with dissatisfaction, discuss other unspoken negative expressions that each has noticed in the other. You might focus on such issues as impatience, skepticism, annoyance, hurt, boredom, and inattentiveness.

Lastly, discuss the positive and negative nonverbal dimensions of such daily routines as the way you enter your home after work, your behavior at meals, and the way you get ready for bed. Review which aspects of these experiences result in closeness and which result in distance. Alert your partner to your nonverbal cues in these contexts so that he or she can "tune in" to your feelings.

NOTE: As a general rule, both verbal and nonverbal means are effective for expressing positive feelings. Negative expressions, which are more apt to be emotion-laden, are best expressed mainly through words. This is important because there is a tendency in delivering a negative expression to avoid responsibility for it:

Frank is angry at Barbara. He glares at her and speaks in a halting, intense manner. When Barbara asks him if something is bothering him, Frank self-righteously maintains that everything's fine.

The sender of most negative, subtle messages has the ability to grumble but will avoid a resolution if confronted by hiding behind the mask of misunderstanding and denial. Therefore, in the interest of clear communication, couples are wise to articulate negative messages so that the sender has responsibility for the message and the receiver can respond unambiguously to the complaint.

THE PRINCIPLE OF DESCRIPTIVE LANGUAGE

The Principle of Descriptive Language: When behavior is described ("I would like you to spend more time with the family") rather than labeled ("You are just plain selfish"), the outcome is likely to be more positive.

===

There is a serious communication malady that at one time or another plagues almost everyone—and at the same time practically all of us are carriers. The malady is called hardening of the categories. Whether or not we are aware of it, we are continually collecting data about other people and our surroundings. We then organize this information in some more or less coherent manner in order to know how to respond. Thus, we are all amateur psychologists; each of us has a theory of personality with which we hope to predict how others will act in their relationships with us.

All too often, in an effort to make sense of what is happening, an overly narrow understanding emerges as a result of labeling complex behaviors and assigning them to a very limited—and limiting—category. On a cultural level, Americans are "mercenary," Germans are "orderly," the English are "distant," the French "passionate," the Italians "emotional"—and so it goes. Rather than capturing the complexity of a culture, this sort of labeling simplistically jams everything into a single pigeonhole. On an ethnic level, blacks are commonly labeled "athletic," Jews "greedy." We even label the sexes—women are "passive," men "aggressive." Again, the totality of the individuals in each of these categories is lost.

Categories are assigned in families also. Freddy, who didn't sleep through the night until he was a year old and began walking at nine months, earns the label "troublemaker." Abbey, another youngster, plays by herself for long periods of time, allowing her busy parents time for themselves. Abbey is labeled the "good child." Another child is considered the "clever one," another "pushy." Many adults have grown up feeling acutely the burden of a label. The "good child," for example, does not always behave desirably, yet he or she is pressured by reputation to suppress the very natural and healthy tendencies to challenge authority, act mischievous, contrary, or angry. Sometimes the labels used are especially destructive. In one instance, a young child is caught shoplifting. His parents, in righteous indignation, impress upon him their judgment that he is a "little thief." Several months later the child is caught stealing again. The parents are shocked. Why so? Isn't stealing what thieves do?

A husband labels his wife a "strong" person who can handle all adversity. Consequently, he becomes distressed on those occasions when she feels anxious and asks for reassurance. The husband's need not to see her as "weak" causes him to ignore her calls for help. Instead, he gets angry or impatient with her, and even adds to her distress by picking on something trivial—to avoid the major issue, her "weakness." The wife then feels there is no one to turn to. Over the years she was continually rebuffed in her efforts for support. Her husband's failure to respond led to her feeling less loved and less loving in return.

Some intimates are convinced that when they use certain labels, they are speaking The Truth. Actually, they have chosen, according to their very personal biases, one of many ways of viewing behavior. To one person, someone who expresses him or herself forcefully is considered a "loudmouth," to another he or she is "spirited." An individual who speaks in a soft tone, smiles frequently, and is careful not to offend may be labeled variously as "tactful," "nice," "evasive," "dishonest," "phony"—depending on the idiosyncrasies of the observer.

Then there are the fluctuations of human behavior. An individual may be sullen one morning, cheerful the next. He or she may be organized one afternoon and in disarray the next. A person may be amorous one evening and the following evening be unresponsive. Categorizing the person implies he or she is always the same. This is hardly ever the case. Indeed, John may act one way while alone, another with his harsh boss at the office; he may behave differently in the sole company of his wife than in the presence of his wife and in-laws;

his behavior may vary with his friends, and on and on as he moves into different contexts. In fact, much of human behavior depends on context—even on such specific variables as how hot and crowded the setting is, or how the furniture is arranged. For example, an arrangement of chairs in a circular configuration is more likely to lead to interaction among participants in a meeting than are other chair formations. Likewise, population density, such as the number of people in a room—is related to certain forms of aggression, regardless of the characteristics of the room's occupants.

The significance of the psychological situation (context) in contrast to fixed personality traits ("he is aggressive," "she is passive") was drastically demonstrated in a simulated prison study conducted in the basement of a psychology department building. College-student volunteers were selected carefully, on the basis of extensive interviewing and diagnostic testing, to have exemplary backgrounds and no antisocial tendencies. Nevertheless, before the close of the week, the stress of being exposed around the clock to what the researchers themselves considered a very realistic simulation of a prison environment resulted in extreme antisocial behavior: brutal harassment and mistreatment of the volunteer "prisoners" by the volunteers assigned to the role of guards. It was evident by the comprehensive screening that the "guards'" reactions were not attributable to more generalized traits (e.g., lack of empathy, rigidity, aggression) existing before they began to play their assigned roles. The potency of the situation, it was concluded, accounted in large part for the untoward conduct. Moreover, once the experiment was over, the "guards" relinquished their aggressive behavior, and all volunteers soon started to respond in terms of the current context of their lives.

All of this is not to say that individuals do not bring personal characteristics—e.g., unique expectations and perceptions—into a situation. However, most of us tend to overemphasize "fixed traits" and ignore the social context. In a relationship, for instance, both partners are constantly influencing one another, so that it is both arbitrary and misleading to interrupt the flow of interaction and assign a singular label or limited category to one person's behavior: "He is over-protective"; "She is sadistic"; "He is hysterical." Labeling and categorizing ignore the very important point that context must be considered. In relationships, the context to be recognized and acknowledged is the interdependence of communication and behavioral exchanges. Quite simply, it is impossible to understand the behavior of one member of a relationship independently of that of the other.

The variations of action-reaction patterns in a couple system are limitless. A very brief sampling includes the man who encourages his partner to speak up, only to interrupt or criticize her when she braves a comment. He interrupts because she provides painfully too much detail. She does so because in previous interactions she felt he too readily misunderstood her point. Both fail to communicate their interactive influence on each other by labeling: he is "rude" for interrupting; she is "timid" for too often remaining silent. Neither has questioned the fact that when she is with her friends—who are encouraging rather than critical—she has no trouble expressing herself.

Another common interactive tangle involves partner A who agrees to complete a task but does not specify when. This provokes the redundant inquiry by partner B, "Did you do it yet?" which is countered by "You're a nag." Partner A is labeled a "procrastinator" and partner B is labeled a "nag." In actuality, partner A does not specify a completion date because he or she fears the consequence of not succeeding; past experiences have been quite unpleasant when a responsibility was not carried out by the specific date. Partner B, on the other hand, feels manipulated and put off by the lack of commitment. As a result, partner B steps up the pressure, which decreases partner A's willingness to complete the task.

Yet another relationship entanglement involves the partner who assigns responsibility to his or her spouse but retains the authority on a final decision. In effect, partner A is told, "You are good enough to do the legwork but the brainy stuff better be left to me." Sometime later, after partner A has been thoroughly defeated by this tactic and begins (justifiably) to resent his or her role, a label of "uncooperative" is assigned and a complaint about "never taking the initiative" is registered.

Based on a report by psychologist Nathan Hurwitz in a *Family Coordinator* report, several additional categorizations that obscure the heart of a matter and impede the change process include:

1. *Interpretations*: "He has an unresolved Oedipal complex."
2. *Pseudo-scientific explanations*: "No wonder she acts that way, she is a Libra. All Libras are flaky."
3. *Psychological name calling*: "He is depressed."
4. *Allegations about intelligence*: "She never could figure things out, and she isn't going to start now!"
5. *Assertions about the ability to change*: "He has a rigid nature. Nothing's going to get him to see things differently."

All of these statements are attempts at classifying a person; even if the categorizations are accurate and fitting, they offer no alternatives or direction for action. What's more, the type of language usually provokes negative emotional reactions in both partners, creates feelings of hopelessness, and often leads to a reactive chain of behaviors that fulfills the prophecy implicit in the statement.

In contrast to the "static" language above is "descriptive" language that reflects the concept of a relationship as fluid and interactive. Descriptive statements, as Dr. Hurwitz advises, address issues in a manner that conveys more fully what is happening (rather than what category a person fits into) and offers a basis for change. Instead of labeling a partner as "depressed," for example, descriptive language emphasizes what the partner is doing, such as sleeping until noon every day. Rather than labeling partner B as "rude," partner A might say, "When I begin to express myself you interrupt with a critical comment." This more expressive language is much preferred because simply saying that a partner is depressed or rude does not indicate what is happening and what can be done about it. Identifying the disturbing behavior is more communicative and provides a starting point for discussion.

A sampling of descriptive comments includes:

1. *Inconsistencies in communication*: "I sometimes question your affection for me because when you say, 'I love you,' you grimace as if it hurt." (Avoid: "You're insincere!")
2. *Commentary about an external factor*: "Since your job change last month, you haven't spent as much time with the family on Sundays as we'd like." (Avoid: "You're just not a family man!")
3. *Explanation of one's own internal states*: "Today, when you started to cry after I called you stupid, I felt guilty, but I acted angry because I thought your crying was a way to control me." (Avoid: "You're just a crybaby!")
4. *Changes in the relationship following a request for a particular event*: "I notice that when you agree to take care of something you are irritable with me for a day or two." (Avoid: "You're only out for yourself!") "Most often when we have an argument I am the one who initiates a truce." (Avoid: "You're inflexible!")
5. *Unknown or difficult-to-define elements in the interactive process*: "I don't know what it is, but very often when we have plans with another couple you start reminding me of my faults, I respond by attacking back, and we go out not speaking to one another." (Avoid: "You're an uptight son of a bitch!")

These examples of descriptive language are not meant to be exhaustive. They are but a sampling that responds to the questions: "What is happening? What is the sequence of events that leads to a displeasing effect?" When answering these questions, marital partners are much more likely to enter into productive dialogue than if they focus on the more limited "What personality trait does my partner have?"

Corrective Prescription

Not only does descriptive language provide a means for communicating more effectively, it also establishes a vehicle for expanding one's own awareness. In this regard, an important element of descriptive language is the expression of one's inner experience. Oftentimes this will convert a confusing or harsh statement into one that is more understandable and acceptable. "I hate you" becomes "My heart is pounding as I say this, but when you make demand after demand of me I feel myself tightening up and wanting to strangle you."

Descriptive messages by their completeness are more likely to convey pain, not merely disdain; descriptive language communicates a desire for resolution, even though the sender may speak of dissolution; descriptive language, because of its thoroughness, signals that the sender is seeking relief, not revenge.

Wife to husband: "When your parents took the children for the weekend, I told you that I was looking forward to being alone with you, and then you invited Joe and Harriet to join us for Sunday. When that happens, I feel hurt and resentful."

Not: "You don't understand me!"

Here is a series of exercises that will help you explore your own awareness and notice some basic properties of your interaction with your partner.

1. The first exercise emphasizes awareness of your inner experiences—what you feel inside your skin, muscular tension, physical manifestations of emotions, discomfort, well-being, and so on.

To begin, close your eyes and just be an observer of your inner life. You may hear your heart beating, the sound of your breathing; you may notice body tension; fantasies may come to your attention. Whatever occurs, don't try to change it, simply become aware. Try beginning a sentence with "Now

I'm aware of" and finish this sentence with your observation of the moment. Continue repeating this sentence and noticing your inner experience for about five minutes.

2. Using descriptive language becomes second nature when we pay attention to our senses. In this exercise using internal sensory data, you are to work with your partner. Face each other and maintain eye contact. Now you are going to tell each other about your outer awareness from moment to moment. Begin by taking turns repeating the sentence "I notice that" and complete the sentence with something that is based on sensory data: an awareness of sound, smell, taste, touch, or sight. For example: "I notice that you have dark circles under your eyes this morning"; "I notice that your hands feel rough"; "I notice that you are wearing perfume," etc. Take five minutes to complete this exercise.

3. Now we are going to combine the previous experience with an exercise using outer awareness, that is, sensory contact with inner events and sensory contact with outside events. Each partner is to describe one pleasing event and one displeasing event, including both his or her inner experience and external observation in the statement. For example, "This morning, when I told you that I was thinking of changing jobs and you told me it was wrong and that I wasn't going about it correctly, I got very upset and began to think you don't see me as being very capable."

4. As you discuss an issue you may discover a series of similar incidents that occur in certain kinds of situations. For example, Ted makes the following observation to Alice: "I've noticed that whenever your parents come to dinner, we start out having a lovely day; but by evening, after they leave, you seem irritable. I don't understand what is happening." Hopefully, Alice will reply with a statement of her experience: "Maybe my folks make me nervous, embarrassed. They're always putting everything down."

Consider one such pattern in your relationship and discuss it using descriptive language. Be particularly aware to include in your comments *your* observation of the interactive effect you and your partner have on each other.

Although descriptive statements at times may seem an unnecessary commentary on the obvious, they are quite important in providing a frame of reference for discussion. What one senses, how one feels, what one thinks, are an endless source of nourishment that opens the door to deeper understanding.

PART V

PART V

Two Can Win: Keys to Conflict Resolution

The German philosopher Arthur Schopenhauer told the story of two porcupines huddled together on a cold winter's night. As the temperature dropped, the animals moved closer together. But then there was a problem: Each kept getting pricked by the other's quills. Finally, with much shifting and shuffling and changing positions, they managed to work out an equilibrium whereby each got maximum warmth with a minimum of painful pricking from the other. Many couples have something in common with the huddling porcupines. They want to achieve and maintain a kind of equilibrium: warmth and closeness but without the sometimes agonizing "pricking" that comes from continuous interaction with another human being.

Some individuals are so desirous of "smoothing the rub" and creating perfect harmony that they keep many grudges hidden from their partner. Unlike those individuals who are excessively and indiscriminately negative, these individuals are unwilling or unable to express their displeasure toward their partner. They are reluctant either to place definite limits on what they will and will not tolerate or to resolve the issues between them. Commonly, their grievance may be rationalized: "Oh, it really doesn't matter anyway"; even the fact that a problem exists may be denied.

In most instances of this sort, withdrawal is chosen rather than confronting the problem and risking a "disturbance of the peace." Often, this occurs because the withdrawing partner has not developed appropriately assertive behaviors; therefore, he or she lacks the ability to express individual preferences or to tell the assertive partner calmly (or not so calmly) of his or her displeasure with the way things are going between them. The assertive partner, on the other hand, compounds the problem further by manipulation, preventing the nonassertive partner from acting on his or her own desires as well. Instead, the nonassertive partner withdraws and fantasizes ways to "get back."

A classic example of underlying and indirectly expressed hostility involves Mr. and Mrs. Herbert Blake, a prosperous suburban couple who have been married for fifteen years. They have two teenaged children and are socially popular. Mr. Blake is an executive with a substantial income; his wife is well dressed, plays excellent bridge, and does more than her share of local charity work. Everybody thinks they have a fine marriage. In addition, both are considered socially desirable, well-informed conversationalists. But at home Mr. Blake rarely says much; to keep the peace, he goes along with whatever his wife wants.

One day shortly after leaving for an all-day charity event, Mrs. Blake returns home unexpectedly for the raffle tickets left on the kitchen table and discovers Herbert in bed with another woman. At first she is incredulous, then horrified. In the marital crisis that follows, Mrs. Blake learns that the "silent treatment" she has been receiving all these years is not cooperation or strength but hostility camouflaged by phony and misleading compliance. Mr. Blake admits that he has never leveled with his wife, never clearly communicated his feelings about the way she dominated most of the family decisions. Though it riled him to no end when she decided what they should do to "have fun or to be creative," almost invariably he went along with her ideas. On the few occasions when he did protest mildly—always without making the true depth of his feelings clear—he found that his wife became even more aggressive. So he became quieter, as he puts it:

"I felt it undignified to get in there and really let her have it. I grew up in a family with a lot of screaming. I remember the hurts, the insults, the pain, and the meanness very vividly. I didn't want that in my life. I didn't want to get embroiled in the kind of rage my parents expressed. Yet being dominated, bossed around, feeling like a doormat, wasn't my cup of tea either. I chose an affair—with a particularly passive woman, by the way—as an equalizer. Taking her to the house, of course, was stupid. Although if I'm going to be brutally honest, I must admit to having mixed emotions about being caught, part of it being, 'Good, you bastard, at least you can unmistakenly see you are not dealing with the village idiot!' I feel curiously relieved."

Not to be confused with an earlier suggestion to increase one's tolerance and leave certain things unsaid—such as remarks that attack a partner's Achilles' heel—the Herbert Blakes among us, both male and female, share a common deceptive belief: It isn't "gentlemanly," it isn't "feminine," to emotionally express dissatisfaction and annoyance; it isn't nice; it isn't mature. This is supposed to be the age of reason, so we must always act civilized and reasonable. Only we don't always feel civilized and reasonable! Ideally, conflict resolution is best if conducted in a harmonious manner, but this need not always be so. Perfect harmony is unrealistic and highly unlikely; simply by sharing space and time together, having different interests and preferences, individuals limit each other's choices. Like the petri dishes of a high school biology class, relationships provide fertile ground in which the germs of conflict can flourish. This does not mean that brawling is being advocated. Rather, conflict—whether deep-seated or superficial—is inevitable and must be recognized. To completely avoid or deny disagreement is a sure way to deaden a relationship.

Some fascinating experiments document this thesis. In the series of famous studies cited earlier, psychologist Harry F. Harlow reared several generations of monkeys and demonstrated that those that were raised by nonfighting monkey mothers would not make love. Another well-known researcher, ethologist Konrad Lorenz, found that birds and animals that did not hold back their aggression became staunch friends. Likewise, Harvard psychologist Erik Erikson and noted psychologist and author George Bach blame the failure to achieve intimacy on the inability to engage in controversy and useful combat.

Today, almost everyone has heard of a separation that seems to be a sudden and unexpected outcome in a tranquil relationship. Of course, this is rarely the case; and a closer look at these relationships reveals not fulfillment, marred by a brief critical crisis, but a profound and cancerous unhappiness resembling that of the characters in Elia Kazan's novel *The Arrangement*. In this story, the protagonist has become increasingly (but quietly) dissatisfied with his marriage, and at forty-three he engages in a serious affair with a younger woman. He is confused by his behavior and feels guilty because he either doesn't understand or won't acknowledge that his wife's good nature is leaving him unfulfilled and conflicted. His wife, true to her helping nature, arranges a plan, a different "style of life" for the two of them, with the hope it will draw them together and rid her husband of his misery. The husband complies—out of passivity or sheer exhaustion—and for almost a year they live in a way designed to protect the couple (him!) from the conflicts that threaten their illusory togetherness. The arrangement, appropriately called the fortress, backfires: Instead of eliminating the husband's marital conflicts, it causes him to become even more passive and, finally, impotent.

During the eleven-month fortress period, the husband and wife are the envy of all their friends. The wife's emphasis on the "pure" life and the husband's surface responsiveness project an image of sharing, togetherness, and unusual devotion. Below the surface, however, is serious conflict, for the dream of "happily ever after" is not shared; it belongs only to the wife. A near-fatal auto accident, which is recognized by the husband as a suicide gesture, forcefully shatters the togetherness fantasy. The husband, after his recovery, leaves his wife.

Perhaps with less drama but through an essentially similar process, many couples grow apart. Although they appear to share common goals, their "arrangement" is based on one person's dream. The other is silently veering off in a different direction. Skillful discussion of disagreement can be the force that prevents the buildup of a fortress; that is to say, every conflict—minor as well as major, long-term as well as brief—involves some emotional reaction. Whether the emotion evolves into alienation or increased intimacy is dependent on how the disagreement is approached. Indeed, the failure to deal constructively with conflict may be the single most powerful force in relationship deterioration.

For some, the "solution" to unresolved conflict is a double life: an emotional divorce from one's partner (preserving the convenience of family life), along with a search for emotional union outside the relationship. The "other man" or "other woman" is sought as a diversion to make a dreary relationship tolerable. The relief is merely temporary and resolves nothing. Sometimes, when a couple have offspring, the relationship may erupt into a war in which the children may be both the ammunition and the primary casualties. Or guerrilla warfare may result, with each partner lunging at the other's weak spots.

Other couples react to their emotional divorce by establishing a pseudorelationship, wherein the satisfaction derived from outside activities masks the emptiness within. Frenzied entertaining and extravagant dining out, frequent residence changing, elaborate decorating, and job hopping can be attempts by the couple to fill the void. Still others engage in major battles in which vicious name calling and sometimes even physical abuse occur. Many relationship battle zigzag through a course of these elements: withdrawal, denial, subterfuge, and out-of-control full-scale attacks. The intention of these futile strategies is to win, to bring down the "enemy."

Conflicts are much more likely to produce positive change when both spouses avoid the trap of taking a win-lose position. In a war there is only one goal: victory. And victory is achieved through destruction. In a relationship the goal of a battle is, hopefully, the opposite: an attempt to improve living conditions and increase closeness. Consequently, to "win" a marital conflict is an illusion; it is an empty victory because it encourages deception in future disagreements ("I'm not about to let him use this against me"), fosters needless pessimism ("What's the use, I can never get my point across, this relationship will never work"), and will very likely lead to retaliation to "even the score."

In some instances, partners may adopt a lose-lose approach. After many disturbing fights, they may give up any hope of individual gain and focus instead on limiting the other's advantage. In essence, then, "winners" are losers because their short-term gain is outweighed by the long-term consequences of relationship erosion. "Losers," in turn, become beneficiaries of lingering bitterness. Rather than being settled, disagreements linger to torture "winners" and "losers."

Both the win-lose and lose-lose positions are fueled by preoccupation with right and wrong. In fact, proclamations of right and wrong are usually arbitrary rules that an individual assigns to his or her preferences. A man, for example, is lying on the couch on a Sunday afternoon watching the football game. His partner attacks him: "How can you lie there all

day! Only an idiot would spend his Sunday in front of the TV."
The man rushes to his defense: "This is my only chance to
relax! Look who's talking anyway, you with your ridiculous
rug-hooking projects." The implication here is that somehow
there is something the matter with the man, he is doing something wrong. His response is, in effect, "I'm OK, there's something wrong with you." The wrong-begets-wrong cycle is
likely to escalate as both parties become further entrenched in
their own truth. Thus, the discussion becomes adversarial and
fixed at the who's right (who wins) / who's wrong (who
loses) level. In actuality, the disagreement, as with most, is
based less on right and wrong than on preference: "I like / I
don't like."

Viewing conflict as arising from differences in preference
rather than "I'm right, you're wrong" can lead to a more collaborative spirit. Frequently, with a win-win posture, brief good-
willed negotiation can settle an issue. In the classic vacation
fight about whether to go to his favorite place or hers, for example, both partners can win either by agreeing to alternate
destinations and flipping a coin to determine whose choice is
honored first, or by seeking a new third possibility agreeable to
both. Here the focus shifts from winning the agreement (defeating the opponent) to concentrating on the issue (defeating the
problem.)

Aside from a willingness to recognize and discuss disagreements and the adaptation of a "two-winner" attitude, a distinct set of skills is needed for successful problem solving. Of
course, it may be apparent by now that the preceding support
and communication principles have definite implications for
problem solving. In fact, their application will prevent or limit
most conflicts. There are times, however, when an issue resists
resolution. Generally, an issue becomes a problem because a
couple have come to an impasse. One or both are emotionally
charged and they cannot reach a mutually agreeable course of
action; even agreeing to disagree proves to be beyond their

grasp. The conflict-resolution principles that follow are a systematized approach designed to resolve just this sort of blockage. Building on a foundation of goodwill and effective communication, these principles represent a multiple-skill approach to arriving at jointly acceptable decisions.

A PRELIMINARY NOTE

Practically everyone has had the experience of wanting to discuss a problem only to find his or her partner unwilling or, worse, downright hostile. When this happens, it is easy to assume that your partner is, at best, uninterested and probably always will be. Occasionally this is the case, and professional consultation may be needed to resolve such a dilemma. More frequently, though, lack of willingness may actually be poor timing. One partner, for example, may have a project he is itching to complete; or a husband or wife may feel out of sorts or be distracted by his or her own worries. The tendency to bring a problem up for discussion when resolution is unlikely can be countered by tabling those issues for a time of day when energy levels are adequate, situating yourselves in pleasant surroundings where distractions are minimized, and allowing ample time—a half-hour minimum—for discussion. Because it is not easy to make these arrangements, it is preferable that a couple view as their first "problem" the making of a "date." The date should include a specific time and setting, and be a prerequisite for more involved discussion.

THE ONE-PROBLEM-AT-A-TIME PRINCIPLE

The One-Problem-at-a-Time Principle: In a problem-solving discussion, only one problem should be discussed. Additional problems or discussions are to be avoided or redirected.

It is very difficult to resolve dissatisfactions when the focus shifts from problem to problem or to irrelevant issues. In international relations, it has long been recognized that smaller contained conflicts are much easier to resolve than larger generalized conflicts. Yet most couples are unaccustomed to a restricted focus. There is a strong tendency to "piggyback" unrelated issues onto a problem-resolution discussion. Requests for change are met with counterrequests, and as a result, a crossed agenda is pursued, which almost always escalates and intensifies the discussion into a personal attack. Diversions, or "sidetracks" as they are usually called, take many forms, as the following examples suggest:

She: You're late.

He: I know, I tried my best.

She: Oh, well! It's just like you to be inconsiderate. Like father, like son.

He: (angrily) What the hell does my father have to do with this?

She: (angrily but controlled) I've seen how he treats your mother: He's late for dinner, he leaves his clothes around, he expects to be catered to. You're the same damn way, and I won't stand for it!

He: (getting louder) You don't say! Who's picking whose dirty underwear off the floor every morning?

She: That's a damn lie!

He: Lie my ass! You're lazy and you know it.

She: (sarcastic) Sure, sure. Keep it up. And what important events occupy you all day, genius?

He: I happen to go to work. What have you got to do all day?

She: I'm trying to get along on the money you don't make, that's what—Mr. Junior Executive.

He: (walking toward the door) Why should I knock myself out for an ungrateful bitch like you?

This couple got very little out of their "kitchen-sink" encounter except a thoroughly spoiled evening. Although the complaint of lateness was legitimate, the issue was diverted when reference was made to a third person, in this case her father-in-law. The complaint became further muddled by the introduction of accusations of sloppiness and laziness; capping the distraction was the attack each launched at the other's daily responsibilities.

Sidetracking often occurs in a more subtle form without either party being aware of it. Consider the following exchange:

Anne: I would like our relationship to include more affection.

Jack: I agree; I would like more affection also.

Anne: It would be good for Martin as well, seeing us being more affectionate.

Jack: Yes, I thought about that also. Seeing us being closer would be an added benefit to our son.

Anne: That's another thing—I feel Martin and I are very close, but that he and you have a distant relationship. I wish you and he could get closer. (sidetrack)

Jack: Well, you know time is really a problem during the tax season . . .

In this exchange, Jack fell into a one-down, defensive trap. In its more intense form, this maneuver is called bait and switch. The diversion begins when one person camouflages his or her true intentions only to engage the partner. When the partner is "hooked," a larger conflict is introduced. It is predictable that the victim of bait and switch will begin to avoid problem solving, perhaps providing the "switcher" with an opportunity to accuse the victim of "never wanting to talk."

Another very common sidetrack is referred to as the scrambled-eggs ploy. When a complaint or relationship issue is responded to with a countercomplaint or counterissue, the problem-solving attempt rapidly becomes scrambled and stunted:

She: I'd like to talk to you about doing your share of the housework.

He: Yeah, we can talk about that when you bring in as much money as I do.

"Low-balling," or adding on extra costs, is the traditional maneuver of the auto salesman, but it is not uncommon in relationships:

He: I think I'll try to get in a few holes of golf this weekend. Do you mind?

She: No, it's all right with me. When are you planning to play?

He: Great. I'll be playing Sunday morning.

She: That's fine. We'll have the rest of the weekend together.

He: Well, not exactly. I am taking a lesson Friday evening. You know how my stroke's been off and I really need to improve. Those guys at the club are really competitive.

She: Well, OK. We still have Saturday.

He: Yes, sure. Part of Saturday anyway.

She: Part?

He: I'm going to the driving range for a few hours Saturday to hit some balls. If I don't practice my swing the lesson will be wasted.

Then there are the drinks and lunch after golf, watching the pros on TV, resting up after a hard weekend of athletics. . . .

Yet another sidetrack, "sinking ship," illustrates the transformation of a problem-solving discussion into an autopsy of a dead relationship?

She: I think you ought to accept the offer of a transfer to Arizona. It's a great opportunity for promotion, and besides, I'm tired of the miserable Chicago winters.

He: You know, it's not really a promotion. The money is the same and the job is actually more difficult. My feeling is I will be isolated from the action.

She: Are you afraid of the challenge? A little work won't kill you!

He: It's not a little work. It's an enormous work load without compensation. I'm sure I was offered the job only because it was turned down by the more senior guys.

She: I'm ready to move and I resent losing the chance because you're afraid of being on your own and facing adult responsibility.

He: That's silly. I am simply considering the problems in the offer.

She: And I am considering the problem in our relationship.

He: Oh, come on.

She: Listen, you know this relationship is hanging on by a thread. You're really straining things unbearably by refusing to move, to give ourselves a fresh start. Either we go to Arizona or we might as well break up.

He: You don't mean it. How can you say that?

She: I do mean it. This relationship needs an infusion of freshness. If you won't cooperate, we are as good as finished.

A particularly troublesome diversion is the attribution of negative motives to a partner's behavior. In most instances, it allows the "malintentioned" to avoid the issue:

Wife: It angered me terribly last night when you told Mike Powers that my sex drive is the product of Victorian upbringing. Our sex life is private! *You were trying to humiliate me.*

Husband: I was not trying to humiliate you.

In this brief exchange, the wife begins by describing a behavior that was upsetting to her. By additionally accusing her husband of bad intentions, she introduces a convenient digression, and the issue is now muddled. The husband feels obliged to defend his intentions and the wife will likely dispute his defense. Often, these conversations end in frustration and a resolution *not* to change:

Husband: (to himself) Why should I censor myself, not talk about my sexual frustration? She will just find another way that I am humiliating her!

Since disputes about what people are feeling and thinking are practically impossible to resolve, attempting to prove negative motives is poor practice. The real issue is the husband's *behavior*, which was troubling, regardless of his *intentions*.

The list of sidetracks and diversions can be as extensive as the imagination is vast. Each is analogous to the "games" psychiatrist Eric Berne described in his popular book *Games People Play*. In discordant relationships, sidetracks are often designed to gain or maintain a position of power. At other times, though, sidetracks may be misguided expressions of commitment to solutions that are genuinely believed to offer mutual satisfaction.

Consider a man's complaint to his partner about her strongly adverse reaction to criticism. The woman responds by pointing out that she becomes upset only when he is critical of her relationship with her parents. Is this a sidetrack? Clearly, she is bringing in a new problem, which has been defined as a sidetrack. Yet, she is also doing something that is a good practice when defining a problem, namely, she is identifying the context in which her distress occurs.

According to phychologists Neil Jacobson and Gayla Margolin in their authoritative text *Marital Therapy*, whether or not this is to be viewed as a sidetrack depends on two factors: first, how it is brought into the discussion; and second, how the discussion proceeds from that point on. If the woman had said, "You're right, I do sometimes become upset and withdrawn when I'm criticized," she would be indicating an acceptance of responsibility for her role in the problem. If she followed this remark by adding, "I think it would be helpful if you recognized that my reaction usually occurs after you've been persistently critical of my contact with my parents," it is clear she would not be trying to change the subject or *blame* her reaction on her partner, but simply providing information that might help them reach a workable solution. In contrast, if her response had been, "You bring on my reaction because of your jealousy," she would be sidetracking, because she would be redefining the problem in a way that implicated her partner as the one who was behaving undesirably.

The discussion should continue to focus on the woman's reaction to criticism rather than on her partner's criticalness. Switching to a discussion of his criticism would be a sidetrack. However, given the new information provided by the woman, the issue of her partner's criticalness should be taken into account in the solution of the problem. Thus, if another problem or issue is mentioned because it relates to the one being discussed, it should not become a new focus. If need be, it can be the focus of a *new* discussion initiated by the person who brought it up.

Corrective Prescription

Below is a list of both constructive and destructive ways to temporarily bring in additional information in order to clarify the issue under discussion. Notice that the primary difference between the two is that sidetracking remarks attribute blame to some *new* factor and imply that this new factor should be the primary focus of discussion.

CONSTRUCTIVE	SIDETRACK
1. I know that I often do not express affection. Sometimes you seem unreceptive, so I avoid rejection. I don't mean to blame you. I'm really just trying to give you an idea of how I restrain myself.	1. If you weren't so cold, I would be more receptive. When are you going to loosen up?
2. You're right. Sometimes I do agree to things and then reneg. Usually, when this happens, I felt coerced to agree in the first place. But reneging is not a good way to show my disagreement.	2. I don't do things because I don't agree with them. They're usually imposed on me. You're too bossy.
3. I apologize for nagging. When you've delayed a task for several days I get frustrated, but I really need to approach the issue differently.	3. If you would complete the tasks in a reasonable time then I wouldn't nag.

In sum, as Drs. Jacobson and Margolin recommend, it is advantageous to acknowledge a relationship between problems. However, couples are discouraged from (1) offering counterrequests for change until the initiator has had an opportunity to express his or her wishes for a change in the other's behavior and the issue has been discussed: (2) insisting that a partner causes the undesirable behavior; or (3) suggesting that the complainer change *before* the complaint can be resolved. Consequently, if a woman brings up a problem, it is *her* agenda and *her* complaint or issue that should be targeted for solution. A related problem can be part of the solution ("To help you change I will . . .") or a topic for additional discussion at a later time.

While it is helpful for intimates to be able to identify their own use of sidetracks, it is often the case that an individual will need "redirection" coaching from his or her partner. This means that the "victim" of the sidetrack should be prepared to

take responsibility for redirecting the exchange in a cooperative manner. To do so requires being able to "slip the punches"
while laying aside the natural but unproductive tendency to
retaliate. Indeed, it is the goal of every manipulation to provoke a response in kind, which sabotages the constructive
effort.

A behavior that would effectively, assertively, and non-
manipulatively redirect sidetracks should contain the following important elements:

1. *Nondefensive bypass*. The temptation to label and
analyze the sidetrack is to be avoided. If Jane were to tell
Jim that his countercomplaining is an attempt to dodge the
issue, Jim is likely to defend himself and escalate the attack.
Ironically, the redirecting effort becomes the diversion.

2. *Positive change*. The redirection statement emphasizes
staying with the issue ("Let's concentrate on getting the
facts") rather than the tendency to shift ("Let's stop trying to
sabotage the discussion").

3. *Empathy*. Acknowledging a countercomplaint or
counterissue is likely to strengthen the redirection effort ("I
can understand how you feel, but . . .").

4. *Repetition*. One of the most critical aspects of redirecting is the willingness to be persistent and to stick to the point
without getting angry, irritated, or loud. Rarely is it necessary
to repeat redirection efforts more than two or three times.

Putting the elements together, here is a successful redirection effort: Jack has acknowledged Anne's complaint about
lack of affection. Anne goes on to accuse Jack of not being
attentive to their son.

Jack: You may be right about that, but let's concentrate
now on expressing affection to each other.

If Anne were to start a round of "sinking ship" by bringing
up another even more serious problem, leading to "this relation-

ship will never work," Jack could offer, "Perhaps there are other problems in the relationship, but now we had best concentrate on ways of expressing our positive feelings more effectively."

In each instance, the diversion is empathically acknowledged without defensiveness or labeling ("You may be right . . . Perhaps there are other problems . . .") and the statement is positive (". . . but now we had best concentrate on ways of expressing our positive feelings . . .").

A reminder: This procedure, as with many of the communication and conflict-resolution directives, assumes an atmosphere of relative goodwill and commitment to the relationship as developed in earlier principles. It may also be apparent that successful redirection efforts require a willingness to put aside false pride and ego indulgences (e.g., games of "I gotcha") in the interest of strengthening the relationship.

THE PRINCIPLE OF DEFINING A DISAGREEMENT

The Principle of Defining a Disagreement: A well-defined problem statement involves a description of the undesirable behavior(s), specifying the situation(s) in which it occurs and the nature of the distress accompanying it. A problem statement is specific, feeling-oriented, responsible, and brief.

Many relationships come to resemble chronic-complaint departments. The same problems are aired repeatedly to no avail. Oftentimes it is not even clear what the point of contention is. The issue may be camouflaged, put forth abruptly, defensively, vaguely, in the form of a lecture, or with hostility.

In all these instances, when a disagreement is defined incorrectly or inadequately, a biasing factor is introduced into each subsequent stage of the problem-solving process.

On the surface, clearly defining a disagreement sounds absurdly easy, and for some few people it is. For many, though, going beyond the basics—he frequently leaves clothes around; she forgets to gas up the car; he hogs the newspaper; she monopolizes conversations—is a skill requiring practice.

It is not uncommon, for instance, to find that the apparent problem rests on an insignificant issue, while the actual gripe is related to something entirely different. A man may nag a woman for being a mediocre housekeeper (even though the housekeeping is only a mild irritant at most) because he is jealous of her professional success. His struggle to achieve has been less than spectacular, and he senses that attacking her on these issues will expose his own feelings of inadequacy and envy. In order to avoid this painful self-disclosure, he chooses (perhaps without being aware of it) to pick on one of his partner's sensitive areas: her housekeeping.

Consider Mr. and Mrs. Smith, a couple who argue regularly about his coming to dinner on time. Mrs. Smith describes the problem quite simply: "My husband is always late for dinner. That's all there is to it." Prompted to discuss the specific sequence of events prior to the dinner hour, Mrs. Smith broadens the perspective:

"At six o'clock, when my husband arrives home, I am in the kitchen putting the finishing touches on dinner. At six fifteen, after washing up and changing his clothes, my husband brings me a whiskey sour and a beer for himself, and we take ten minutes out for a drink. There is usually some pleasant talk of the day's happenings, and my husband usually gets himself another beer. Typically, I suggest he give me a hand in the kitchen rather than finishing his second drink alone. And, typically, he grumbles about my suggestion while I go back into the kitchen muttering some angry thoughts about equality and all that stuff.

"Then comes six forty-five. Dinner's ready and on the table. I call once, no answer. Twice, 'Yeah, I'm coming.' Five minutes later I go into the TV room enraged and tell him that dinner's cold and he's an inconsiderate bastard.

"Now he comes. We eat in silence, we don't even exchange glances. After dinner we soften, he even helps with the dishes occasionally. That is our dinner routine."

Looking at the more detailed pattern, it is apparent the problem involves more than remedying a "simple case of tardiness." Mrs. Smith acknowledges that beckoning her husband repeatedly doesn't work, yet she plays out her part in the dinner-time drama in exactly the same manner each evening. How is it that Mrs. Smith doesn't tire of being rejected in her bid for help? And couldn't Mrs. Smith call her husband several minutes before dinner was ready? Certainly, this seems an obvious solution. How did she miss it? Is there some sort of payoff Mr. and Mrs. Smith derive from their behavior?

Scrutinizing her actions, Mrs. Smith realizes that, in fact, she does not want her husband's help in the kitchen even though she requests it on cue each evening. This becomes apparent when Mrs. Smith asks herself what she wants her husband to do in the kitchen. In actuality, she would rather do everything herself. By asking her husband to help out, Mrs. Smith is really fishing for a statement of appreciation for her *own* efforts. Reluctantly, Mrs. Smith also recognizes that her husband's rejection affords her the opportunity to feel "one-up" by badgering him with his uncooperativeness.

While his wife bemoans her fate, Mr. Smith expresses his resentment and wrestles out of his "one-down" position through noncompliance: "Let her call me, it serves her right for asking me to help after a hard day's work. I'll show her who's in charge here." The dinner-time dilemma is now redefined. Mrs. Smith wants to feel appreciated and respected, Mr. Smith wants the same. The evening meal simply became a convenient—and misleading—arena.

In some instances, the quarrel may be somewhat more on

target, but the issue continues to be clouded. Adam and Becky are a couple in their mid-thirties. Adam is a journalist for a metropolitan newspaper whose work often stretches into twelve or fourteen hours daily. Becky has a part-time crafts business, which she runs out of their home. The issue focuses on the disbursement of money to their preadolescent daughters.

Adam: I think the girls are too free with money.

Becky: I don't know, they seem pretty sensible to me.

Adam: I'm not saying they're bad kids; it's just that they are not realistic about money matters. They don't really have a sense of value.

Becky: Oh, I'm sure they'll learn soon enough.

Adam: Becky, I think you're spoiling them. You're too free with money. They get the impression from you that it comes easy.

Becky: You spend money pretty freely yourself. Why don't *you* set a better example?

Adam: That's the point!

Becky: It damn well is. When the kids see you spending money like Mr. Big Spender, it influences their behavior.

Adam: Well, you may be a more conservative shopper than I am, but that is not the point.

Becky: I don't know what the point is—you're blaming me for their behavior!

In their dialogue, Adam actually bypassed his feelings and ended up getting mired in a nonissue. Here is his position restated:

Adam: Becky, I am feeling as if I don't count with the kids anymore. Partially, I think that's due to my heavy work load. But, when you counter our mutual decisions, such as increasing the kids' allowances, without discussion, it intensifies my feelings.

Becky: You're right. You're not around enough and you don't know their needs.

Adam: I understand that does make things more difficult. But I want to be part of the decision-making process with them even if it requires extra effort.

Becky: What kinds of decisions are you referring to? You don't think I should consult you on every minor detail, do you?

Adam: Of course not. What I would like to discuss further are some guidelines for curfews, allowance, sleeping over at a friend's house, and the like. This way I can feel more a part of the household.

In this replay conversation, Adam includes a statement of his feelings; he openly acknowledges his part in the problem; he makes a specific observation about unilateral decision making. This type of remark sets the tone and direction for productive discussion.

The goal in the initial phase of conflict resolution is defining the problem clearly; *both partners must have descriptions of the undesirable behavior, the situation in which the problem occurs, and the consequences of the problem for the partner who is distressed by it.*

Corrective Prescription

The function of a well-defined problem statement is (1) to provide a guide to discussion by describing what needs to be remedied; (2) to enable a couple to know when they have found a remedy, since the solution should match the problem formulation.

As we have seen, the "real" problem can sometimes be elusive. The following guidelines, taking this factor into account, have been developed to increase the likelihood that objectionable behaviors will be defined accurately and in a manner that lends itself to resolution. Nonetheless, it would be well to review the Direct-Communication Principle before initiating a problem-definition discussion.

1. In beginning a problem discussion, first answer the questions: What is it that your partner *does* or *says* that you want changed? Or, what would you like from your partner that you are not getting? Under what circumstance or in what context is the change wanted? (For example, if a man wants an increase in expressions of appreciation, which of his behaviors does he want recognized? Are there times and places he prefers the acknowledgment be made?)

The responses to these questions provide a helpful directive only if the language emphasizes specifics—behaviors that can be heard or seen, contexts that are clearly described. It is here that the Principle of Descriptive Language is usefully applied.

In the same vein, avoid negative labels. Not only do these terms obscure specificity, but they are provocative. Compare "you are a cold person" with the more descriptive "I would like you to kiss and hug me more often." The former is likely to be sharply rebutted ("Look who's talking, Miss Frigid!"), the latter is often negotiable. If an individual consistently relies on derogatory labels, it is likely that problem resolution is not a priority; rather, it is the expression of anger and revenge that leads the agenda.

2. It's important to make your feelings known ("I feel rejected when you don't include me in your plans"). Expressions of feeling are quite powerful and constitute an important element in a message: the effect of the displeasing behavior. When the feelings underlying relationship dissatisfaction are expressed in an honest, responsible manner, it is more likely that the listener will be responsive. The "I Message" Principle has particular application here.

3. Avoid the "always-never" messages so common in discordant relationships. This overgeneralization dilutes the precision of a statement and diverts the discussion away from the problem. Whether the problem occurs "all" of the time or *some* of the time, it is a problem. Debates about frequency usually lead nowhere.

4. Brevity is an aid to problem definition. During the initial

period of discussion in particular, it is wise to avoid giving numerous and lengthy examples of the problems; excursions into the past for causes of the problems serve no constructive purpose. "I will not buy a new car because I was brought up in poverty" makes little difference in reaching agreement with your partner on what to do about the old car.

While connections between childhood events and current behavior do not usually add to a problem formulation, immediate or current reactions often do increase understanding. "I am afraid to initiate sex because I do not want to be rejected" provides valuable information and should be mentioned as long as the discussion remains on the defined problem, not the explanation.

5. A law of physics states that every action has an equal and opposing reaction; correspondingly, every problem is an interaction between *two* people. For example, there can be no dominating husband without a submissive wife, no interrupting wife without a passive and willing husband. Every "villain" requires a cooperative "victim." Consequently, when discussing a problem, it is good policy to state your *own* role in the problem as well as your partner's. Although the focus is to remain on your partner, collaboration is best accomplished when responsibility for a problem is shared.

6. For those couples who complain of excessive mutual criticism, it is often useful to begin a problem discussion with a positive comment: "You are very communicative during dinner and I would really love it if you were more talkative in the morning." The positive statement reminds your "battle-worn" partner that you recognize and appreciate his positive behavior. Further, the discipline of expressing a positive before a negative comment may give pause for thought, allowing time for you to reconsider expressing petty criticisms *before* they are expressed.

7. Lastly, it is *not* advisable to suggest to one's partner that the issue being brought forward is not the "real" problem. Most often this leads to an interminable and painful analysis

of each individual's character, which cannot be verified. On the other hand, proceeding with the guidelines above and the conflict-resolution principles to follow will yield a result that can then be more clearly judged by its effect on the relationship.

So that the Conflict-Resolution Principles may be applied, a list of potential areas of conflict follows. Each partner is to choose one of these issues (or add one specific to your relationship) and develop the issue as suggested above. This same issue is to be carried to resolution with each succeeding Conflict-Resolution Principle.

Flip a coin to determine which partner is to go first. If partner A wins the toss, he or she is to take his or her problem through each step of conflict resolution. Only after partner A completes his or her turn does partner B begin the process.

Relationship behaviors for discussion:

Decisions about spending money
When and how to have sex
Discipline of children
Expressions of affection
Working late
When and where to take vacations
How and when to entertain friends
Division of household responsibilities (e.g., preparation of meals, payment of bills, etc.)
Shared time together
Activities apart from each other
Activities of family as a group
Decisions about religious practices
How and when to entertain in-laws
Taking an interest in the furnishing of the home

THE BRAINSTORMING PRINCIPLE

The Brainstorming Principle: It is often beneficial in the initial stage of problem solving to generate a list of solution possibilities without clarification and without evaluation of their merits.

It is not surprising that behavioral scientists relate the breakdown of "change" conversations to the attitude that there is only one solution to a conflict. What's more, it is fairly common for each partner in a relationship to see only one possible solution to a dilemma: his or her own. The stress of conflict or even of anticipated conflict is actually quite conducive to rigid adversarial positions among couples:

Pete: I would like you to be interested in sex more frequently.

Louise: I hardly ever say no to you.

Pete: That's true, but you're there in body, not spirit. You go along with my initiative, but when you're not into it, I feel frustrated.

Louise: I like making love to you. It's just that sex is not as important to me. I'd prefer to get together less frequently.

Pete: Well, how come you were so much more interested before we were married? I feel you projected a false image of yourself.

Louise: Oh, come on. There was novelty and less responsibility, we were both in different states of mind, and life was less complicated. Who can continue at the same passionate pace after a decade of marriage?

Pete: What's so complicated about your life that's made you less interested in sex?

Louise: I'm interested in starting a career, developing my own identity.

Pete: But I want to have sex more frequently.

Louise: I understand, but what am I supposed to do if I don't feel like having sex every time you do?

In many relationships, differing sexual desires are a continual issue. Few people have equal sex drives or even the same affectional needs; the more active partner often feels frustrated, the less active partner is frequently nagged by guilt. Rather than pollute their relationship with a pattern of resentment and withdrawal, Pete and Louise develop the following list of possible solutions:

Pete will stop equating refusal with personal rejection.

Louise will begin reading and viewing erotic material in an effort to become more sex-oriented.

Pete will rely on masturbation more often.

Pete will have an affair.

Louise will have an affair (!).

Pete will not judge Louise's sexual responsiveness.

Pete and Louise will each take responsibility for introducing more variety in their lovemaking.

Pete and Louise will talk more about their sexual thoughts and preferences.

Pete and Louise will both initiate more nonsexual snuggling and gestures of affection.

Louise will initiate sex more often.

Pete will be more helpful to Louise so that she can direct more of her energies toward sexuality.

Using this list, Pete and Louise have a broader array of possibilities to discuss. They are less likely to reach a premature impasse, become diverted into a battle of who's right, and go to bed angry. Indeed, it is not unusual for an issue that has been "brainstormed" to take on a significantly more positive tone.

For instance, a couple might argue endlessly about the frequency of their sexual contacts when, in fact, the heart of the matter may be the desire of one partner for more affection, reassurance, or security. The issue may linger at the more superficial level of sexual frequency because it is poorly thought out; or perhaps the issue is easier to discuss than the more delicate matter of feeling undesirable, unattractive, or unsure about the relationship. Brainstorming, by opening the discussion to various alternatives, allows for this exploration. Increasing the sexual desires of one person or reducing those of the other—an arduous task at best—now takes on a broader meaning. Feelings of reassurance and desirability can be enhanced in any number of ways. Sexual behavior is only one—and often not the most important.

Brainstorming can be applied to almost any problem. Consider as another example Aileen and Henry, who have difficulty because Henry's involvements with business, friends, and athletics keep him away from home too much of the time. After brainstorming, they arrive at the following list of possibilities:

Henry will give up two nights a week for a "date" with Aileen.

Aileen will work with Henry part-time.

Aileen will participate in more of Henry's interests, such as athletics.

Henry will give up his more casual social relationships.

Henry will invite his friends to his home with their spouses.

Aileen will meet Henry for lunch during the week.

Henry and Aileen will plan several weekends away alone during the year.

Aileen will pursue more of her own interests.

Henry and Aileen will accept spontaneous invitations from each other.

From this list of solutions, Henry and Aileen can begin to eliminate those that are impractical or otherwise undesirable and retain those that warrant closer consideration.

Corrective Prescription

It is often the case that having too few alternatives from which to choose leads a couple to feeling trapped. In these instances, resolution is likely to be unilateral—imposed by one partner—and unsatisfactory. In contrast, if a couple allow a free exchange of ideas, an encounter without consequences, their gain is a truly shared problem-solving effort. The brainstorming guidelines that follow provide for this collaborative experience by suspending the threat of disagreement and suggesting that differing views can be a basis for developing creative alternatives. Herewith are guidelines for brainstorming sessions.

1. *Don't evaluate.* Evaluation is likely to inhibit the suggestion of possibilities; brainstorming is best viewed as a time to suspend judgment. Statements such as "That will never work," "That's silly," "That doesn't make sense," and even more encouraging remarks such as "That's a terrific idea" are to be avoided.

2. *Don't clarify or seek clarification.* Brainstorming involves the rapid generation of ideas; explanations tend to impede the process. Clarification and explanation are appropriate only after a list of alternatives is developed. Many couples are strongly tempted to contaminate their brainstorming with irrelevant (or at least premature) information, such as examples and explanations. Since a conflict resolution will ultimately be derived from the options created by brainstorming, it is important to avoid this trap; each partner can assist the other in this effort by gently redirecting digressions. A remark like "I see what you mean but let's just generate a long list of ideas now" is often a sufficient reminder.

3. *Don't censor.* Sometimes what appears at first glance to be a far-out or silly idea may provide the stimulus for an innovative or unconventional solution. In one instance, a wife

suggested to her business-troubled husband that they simply pick up and start anew. Although they didn't leave town permanently, both decided to take a much needed vacation so that business dilemmas could be brought into perspective. Upon returning, the husband, sparked by his wife's support ("I'm in this with you all the way") was able to take the risks required to get his business in order.

In addition to providing an opportunity for going beyond the idea being suggested by adding to it or combining it with other ideas, uncensored, "zany" input serves as a relaxant that can foster creativity.

4. *Record each idea.* Most of us have had the experience of thinking "that's a really interesting idea" only to forget it soon afterward. To avoid this, ideas should be written down; each partner should have access to the written list both during and after the brainstorming session. In keeping with the noncritical atmosphere of brainstorming, all ideas should be listed together rather than being divided into "his" and "hers" lists.

5. *Refine and eliminate.* In the latter stage of brainstorming after a list of alternatives has been generated, clarification, refinement, and elimination take place. What remains is a list of reasonable solutions that can be discussed at greater length.

It is critically important at this juncture that substantive issues are not confused with relationship issues; that is, rejection of one's partner's suggestion should not be interpreted as rejection of that partner, only of the suggestion. The goal in problem solving is to develop a lasting, durable solution; ownership of a particular suggestion is immaterial. The question is "Will it work?" not "Whose idea was this?"

THE PRINCIPLE OF MUTUALITY
AND COMPROMISE

The Principle of Mutuality and Compromise: Both partners are affected by and involved in a problem; consequently, solutions should involve change on the part of each partner.

When an atmosphere of trust and goodwill is developing and communication is becoming more skillful, individuals are in a good position to bargain, negotiate, and work at compromises in their relationship. To some people, "bargaining" and "negotiating" are terms to be applied to business, not relationships. In relationships, writers of popular magazine articles argue, people should "make sacrifices," "give for giving's sake," "do it for him," "be more loving," etc. These admonitions ignore the fact that most people have different tastes, attitudes, behaviors, and goals, and that these differences can be resolved only on the basis of mutually understood "rules of exchange."

Charles and Joan, a couple in their late twenties, operate within the framework of what might be described as a "traditional" marriage. Joan is considerate of and expresses her affection for Charles, takes primary responsibility for the children, prepares meals, and cleans the house. When asked why she does these things, Joan replies, "Because I love Charles."

Joan may indeed love Charles, but she engages in these behaviors in exchange for certain behaviors from Charles. He is considerate of her and expresses his affection for her; he provides their income, makes household repairs, and takes care of the cars. If these behaviors were to stop, would there be a change in Joan's behavior? Quite likely. Very rarely are individuals so complementary in tastes and desires that negotiating and compromising are not required. For the rest of us, scores of conflicts are inevitable unless we have a good understanding of what our partners expect to get and give in return. When this understanding is lacking or the giving and getting cease to be reciprocal, bitterness, resentment, and general unhappiness usually result.

Morris and Evelyn have been married for four years. For the first three years of their marriage, they both work, Morris as an engineer, Evelyn as a teacher. During those three years, Morris and Evelyn share a common goal—purchasing a home—which they accomplish. At the end of their third year of marriage, two things happen: Evelyn gives birth, and Morris receives a substantial promotion. As a result of these events, Morris and Evelyn experience a dramatic change in their usual routine. Evelyn leaves her teaching position and is at home all day caring for her child. Morris is home less because of his increased responsibility. When Morris returns home, he is sometimes irritable and usually quite fatigued. Often, he is greeted by a wife who feels equally off-color. To prepare himself for the unpleasant news and growing friction at home, Morris begins stopping for a drink after work. Evelyn, disgusted with the unpredictability of his arrival home, stops preparing meals. Morris, in turn, begins eating out more frequently. As a result, they become more and more distant:

Morris: It used to be that we sat down, had cocktails and a leisurely meal together. We would discuss our day and enjoy each other's company. Then I came home and the house was a mess, the meal was lousy, and I was greeted by a tiger ready to lunge at me.

Evelyn: I felt Morris no longer had any interest in me. He seemed to have more interest in his business. When he came home, all he wanted to do was eat quickly, watch TV, and go to sleep. When I suggested that we go out together after the baby went to sleep, he constantly refused because he was tired.

Well, I was tired also, but I desperately needed some stimulation.

Morris: We seemed to have lost our coordination. For example, with sex, Evelyn felt that I was interested only when I was horny, and unresponsive to her needs when she felt sexy. As a result, we hardly had sex anymore.

Both Evelyn and Morris feel they aren't getting a just return for their efforts. Morris feels that his difficulties in coping with the pressures of his new position aren't appreciated. Evelyn feels that Morris does not recognize the difficulties of her adjustment. Day after day, night after night, both Evelyn and Morris seek to exert power over each other, to reap his or her "fair share." Fortunately, having a sound relationship and the basis for good communication, they eventually see the futility of their struggle and agree to work things out through compromise. Their attitudes sitting down together can be characterized thus: "I can't have everything I want and you can't have everything you want, so let's compromise in such a manner that we each have those things that are most important, and at the same time let us each try to foster the well-being of the other to the maximum extent possible."

Sadly, most couples are either unaware of such a workable "exchange attitude" or merely pay it lip service. As a result, their many differences with regard to food preferences, moods, sex, types of entertainment, choice of friends, responsibility for household tasks, personal habits (e.g., smoking and drinking), and employed activity (e.g., working late or on weekends) are a constant source of friction. The message they convey to each other seems to be "If you won't change for me, then I won't change for you." In contrast, those couples who live by the tenets of mutual exchange—compromise, recognition of individuality, and compassion—are more likely to discuss issues of conflict, not as adversaries but as partners, and thus avoid endless unnecessary bickering. The message they convey to each other seems to be "You scratch my back and I'll scratch yours."

Here are some of the agreements Evelyn and Morris worked out: Evelyn agrees not to "close in" on Morris as soon as he arrives home but to allow him time to shower and take a short nap. Evelyn arranges for a babysitter and is also able to nap and refresh herself in the early evening. They both agree to eat a late dinner together after the baby is asleep. One night a week is set aside for going out for dinner and entertainment.

During their discussions, Morris recognizes that Evelyn's moods and behaviors are greatly influenced by his acknowledging her as a capable homemaker and desirable wife, and that this acknowledgment needs to go beyond the form of a mere statement made to himself; it would most effectively be a personal demonstration that he loves and admires her as a person, and that she is as important to him as his work. Morris's plan includes two elements: expressing his appreciation of Evelyn more often and increasing his involvements in household responsibilities, including sitting down with Evelyn and working out tactics for making life easier.

Morris also suggests to Evelyn that if their relationship does not improve as a result of the numerous exchange agreements, he will consider changing to a less demanding job. Evelyn is profoundly touched by Morris's offer. She recognizes the signficance of his statement and tells him so. She adds that his interest and appreciation make her work more acceptable and a job change is unnecessary. She also begins to express more interest in his work.

Whenever applicable, a disagreement or conflict with some aspect of your partner's behavior should be approached by offering to change some aspect of your *own* behavior. Mutuality is more effective than unilateral change attempts because most of us find changing more acceptable if we aren't doing it alone. In addition, one partner's change (Evelyn's agreement to give Morris some private time when he arrives home) makes it easier for the other partner to change (Morris's agreement to abstain from an after-work stopover for a drink).

Sometimes, the mutuality may be in the form of one partner offering him or herself in the service of the other partner's change efforts. This is illustrated by Morris's offer to sit down with Evelyn in an effort to work out tactics for household management. Contrast this with the partner who chronically complains about a messy house and lousy meals but never puts forth a constructive suggestion for remedying the displeasure.

There are several types of negotiating and compromising situations. One is meeting-in-the-middle-ground: being reconciled to buying a medium-priced car rather than either the expensive sports car or the economy compact, or agreeing that one partner will limit his or her drinking to one per evening when the drinking partner would like three drinks an evening and the other prefers he or she doesn't drink at all. A second type of compromise involves trading: Alice is paying the bills in return for Tom's keeping the cars maintained.

Another type of negotiating is one that is not immediately time-bound. In this instance, the couple recognize that if one spouse does something for the other, the benefited spouse need not *immediately* turn around and pay off the debt. It is assumed on good faith that there will be an opportunity for reciprocity in the future.

One couple, Lois and Ron, face the problem of a career conflict. Ron is an engineer, Lois is an attorney specializing in corporate law. They both have jobs in Boston and are simultaneously offered new positions, Lois in Chicago, Ron in Dallas. In both cases, the new jobs appear to be just what they are looking for individually. But if they are to continue their relationship, one of them will obviously have to defer to the other's needs. The position offered Lois gives her an opportunity that simply cannot be duplicated anywhere else in the country. And while Ron's job offer is an extremely good one, there exist a number of other engineering firms doing similar work, two of which are in the Chicago area. So, after discussing the options open to each of them, Ron concedes that his opportunities are more flexible in Chicago than Lois's are in Dallas. He agrees to go to Chicago, where Lois can begin her exciting opportunity. Within six weeks of their arrival in Chicago, Ron finds a job that is the equivalent of the one he was offered in Dallas.

This kind of arrangement, based on the assumption that if there comes a time in their lives when their positions are reversed, the other partner will likewise compromise, is ideal. As with most idealistic promises, though, it works best under ideal conditions: well-functioning relationships involving a high degree of trust and reciprocity. When one spouse continues to imply or promise that he or she will do something in the future but never gets around to it, or when one person has an extremely selective memory—recalling all his or her contributions but none of the partner's—relationship discord and bitterness are the predictable outcome.

Corrective Prescription

Whenever differences occur, whether between intimates, business partners, or nations, they are resolved in only three ways: one party attempts domination (result: hostility, war); there is mutual or unilateral withdrawal (result: divorce, isolation); there is mutual compromise (result: exchange, goodwill). If individuals are seeking a more satisfying relationship with each other rather than divorce or aggression, mutual exchange and compromise clearly offer the greatest promise.

A major deterrent to effective negotiating is the tendency to view the partner's behavior in all-or-nothing terms. Kevin, an outgoing, verbal man, demands that Pam, a quiet, very private person, talk about her feelings every day. Marsha expects Fred, who is often forgetful and avoids responsibilities, to fulfill all his responsibilities on time and without reminders. Susan insists that Alan increase his time with his son by playing with him before and after work.

Demands for sweeping changes practically always overwhelm the recipient and result in a refusal. Consider another strategy recommended by psychologists Neil Jacobson and Gayla Margolin, as well as by other leading therapists. Begin with less than what is ideally desired but with a suggestion or plan that is more likely to be acceptable to your partner. Later, if the degree or change proves to be insufficient, further negotiations can occur. The change or preference request can be formulated in two ways:

1. What do I ideally want?
2. What am I willing to accept for the present?

For example, consider the husband who, as far as his wife is concerned, spends an insufficient amount of time playing with their two-year-old son. The wife ideally wants him to spend some time each morning before work and each evening after work with his son. The husband agrees that he should spend more time with their son but complains that mornings are too rushed for quality interaction. The wife is willing to accept her husband's offer to spend at least a half hour playing with their child each evening. This couple's agreement, based on a reduced request, may work out quite satisfactorily; if not, at some future time it may be renegotiated. However, since movement has already occurred in a positive direction, additional requests are less likely to be overwhelming.

Here are some additional suggestions for negotiating and compromising moderately abrasive differences before they become severe:

1. At this juncture, mutual agreement that the communication skills discussed earlier are adequate and operative is a definite prerequisite. Without this, bargaining is very likely to break down and worsen rather than improve the relationship. If after a reasonable period of attempting to improve communication skills there is no progress, professional help should be considered.

2. As usual, choose a time and make a formal appointment with each other for the compromise-exchange discussion. Pick an hour when interruptions are unlikely. An ideal time is when both partners will be unhurried and relaxed. If there are several postponements of meetings, this may be an indication that one or both partners are avoiding a confrontation. Discuss this issue.

3. Remember, as discussed in the Direct-Communication Principle, each spouse should state very specifically what he or she would like or desire. For example, "I would like greater closeness" is too vague and general. More specific statements that would be instructive to a mate might be "I would like to eat dinner together" or "I would like to spend time each evening discussing the day's events."

4. Begin with what is wanted rather than what is not wanted. Since both partners may have the tendency to use the exchange session as a forum for condemning the other, it is wise to focus on increasing desired behavior until confidence in the procedure and in each other is established. For example, "I would like more statements of appreciation" is positive, whereas "I want you to stop picking on me as you have been" may lead to an argument. Avoid evaluative, right-and-wrong types of statements. Consider differences as just what they are: differences.

5. Avoid using outside standards to express what is wanted. There is less likelihood of resistance when other people's standards are not used as levers. For instance, rather than saying "Why can't you be like Ed Jones?" simply state what you want without the comparative reference.

6. When the change requested is outside the behavioral repertoire of a partner, steps to improve or gain the behavior should include a plan for mutual involvement. For example, if both decide that the wife needs more schooling to increase her earning power, perhaps the husband will take on additional household responsibilities to make this feasible.

7. Do not try to negotiate feelings. Feelings are not usually changed by bargaining; "Okay, I agree to be happy about vacationing with your parents" just won't work. Only behaviors can be negotiated; and only those behaviors that do not compromise a person's integrity are open to negotiation.

8. One of the difficulties that may occur in negotiating differences involves communicating the importance of a particular preference or issue. In this regard, particularly for the less complex issues, using a zero-to-ten rating scale to indicate the relative strength of a preference can prove useful. (Zero represents total disinterest or displeasure; ten signifies total enjoyment, enthusiasm, agreement). For example, a man may want his partner to attend a work-related function with him. His partner may opt for a party given on the same evening in honor of their next-door neighbors who are moving away. Using the rating scale (he gives his function a six, she gives the neighbors' party a nine), each is provided with an immediate and clear-cut idea of the strength of the partner's feelings; in this manner, many confusing, nondirective statements are eliminated: "I want to if you want to . . . but do you really mind . . . Well, maybe we shouldn't . . . I don't care, it's up to you. . . ."

The rating scale is particularly useful for couples who have difficulty expressing the intensity of their preferences. Use of a rating scale, however, should not put an arbitrary end to the matter being discussed. It is best used as one ingredient to consider in the overall discussion of differences. What's more, rating requires making an honest appraisal; strong-willed or manipulative individuals who consider most of their preferences as tens will soon find their partners unreceptive to this suggestion.

9. Be patient. Compromise-and-exchange agreements are difficult. Do not expect to arrive at a mutual agreement immediately. Several discussion sessions may be necessary, even

---

on seemingly minor issues. Severe and long-lasting differences may require professional assistance for successful resolution.

THE PRINCIPLE OF CLARIFYING AND SUMMARIZING THE FINAL AGREEMENT

The Principle of Clarifying and Summarizing the Final Agreement: Once agreement has been reached, each party should clearly state what he or she is going to do differently.

Practically all social relationships involve agreements—whether official or unofficial, tacit or explicit—that govern the ways in which people behave toward each other. In marital relationships, where contact is frequent and covers a wide variety of behaviors, agreements are particularly important. Official agreements, those sanctified by state or religious institutions, usually address the general structure of the marital relationship: the duty to "love, honor, and obey." In those instances where the parties' rights and obligations, as well as provisions for sanctions in the event of noncompliance, are specified, couples usually ignore them until confronted by the possibility of divorce.

Unofficial agreements, those developed by the marital partners themselves, are usually taken more seriously, since they are concerned with the specific business of daily living—how each partner will behave toward the other, as well as the assignment of responsibilities. Some of these agreements are explicit and mutually understood. A man, for instance, may suggest that he will do the food shopping and, in exchange for his effort, take a few hours for himself later on to play ball. A woman may agree to take care of certain chores if other family members will cooperate with her in specified ways. All families have rules—a series of agreements—that dictate those actions to be rewarded and those to be ignored or punished.

While some agreements are verbalized, many remain unvoiced. A husband badgers his wife; and when she's had as much as she can take, her hands begin to tremble. He continues pushing, only to propel them into a ferocious battle, followed by withdrawal. After this sequence has been repeated a few times, both "know" that trembling hands are a signal to back off. Sex—where to have it, the type of sexual behavior engaged in, as well as frequency—is another common area of unspoken agreement. Partners often signal each other ("When he shuts the TV before the late news I know he's interested") in this sensitive area. Sometimes the division of responsibilities also falls into place without a spoken agreement. Whether by convention ("man's work," "woman's work"), competence (each person doing those things he or she does best), availability, or some other standard, decisions may be made without discussion.

Some types of relationship "contracts," as agreements are often called, are made with no intention of carrying out the agreed-upon terms. One particularly destructive variation involves the making of an offer that is withdrawn when a partner accepts. In the language of Dr. Eric Berne, the bid for a contract by the first person is a "setup," the switch in midstream is termed a "coup," and the entire fraudulent transaction is a "game." For example, early in the week, a husband may suggest that he take a day off so that he and his wife can share intimate time together. The wife, having already made plans for the week, nonetheless consents enthusiastically so that she does not discourage such offers in the future. Her acceptance is met with an accusation rather than appreciation: "How could you be so unconcerned with my career progress to encourage my absence from work!" Berne termed games of this sort "RAPO."

Illicit contracts such as the one described above can create agony and will most often spawn more of the same. The wife, having been wounded, may devise a game of her own to retaliate. The end result is frequently a contract that results in mutual avoidance—a maneuver which, if continued, often evolves into the more formalized contract of divorce.

Most of the agreements that direct a couple, however, are both effective and constructive. What's more, it is neither necessary nor desirable that each and every agreement between a couple be discussed. Not only would the process be cumbersome, encompassing literally thousands of interactions between a couple, but it could become a source of embarrassment and conflict. When Jared offers to do the shopping in exchange for ball-playing time, his wife may feel hurt that he isn't shopping "simply to please me." Or, if Jared and Lorraine have silently agreed that he is the one to initiate sex by shutting the TV at a certain hour, the expression of this agreement may cause embarrassment. It is only when there is some disagreement or unhappiness with an arrangement that agreements need to be explicitly specified.

In those instances where a couple have been disturbed by a conflict and enter into problem solving, they are often so elated about reaching an agreement that they fail to work out the nitty-gritty details of how the solution will be implemented. This is most unfortunate because a solution is no better than its implementation; critical to implementation is a clear understanding of who will do what and by when. If couples do not specify the nature of the changes to be made and delegate the responsibility for these changes, or if the terms of the agreement are vague, it is quite likely that chaos and discouragement will result.

A very common and deceptively mild agreement breakdown is demonstrated by the person who agrees to a particular problem solution but fails to follow through. For example, a man may agree that he does not give the relationship sufficiently high priority, that he is neglectful of his partner's desire to have him as a companion. As one part of the solution, the man agrees to pick up ballet tickets that evening, an expression of his relationship-concern. But he "forgets"; and since he breaks his promises chronically, his partner's disappointment triggers an ugly battle. For some people, being unreliable becomes a way of life. Frequently, these are individuals who are motivated by temporary feelings of guilt ("He seems so upset about my not being attentive") or who require the approval of their partner ("I better say yes; she seems terribly mad about this"); others simply acquiesce to "get the nag off my back." The relief is usually shortlived, only to be replaced by their partner's rage.

A predictable progression of the "forgetful" partner involves the man or woman who intentionally avoids specifying a time when the agreement will be honored. This may take the form of "Yes, I will get the tickets." The recipient of this agreement is left temporarily appeased; but if compliance is repeatedly delayed, a negative cycle of nagging and coercion is likely to pollute the relationship. The same effect is often produced by other vague agreements: "I agree that I need to be more attentive" or "Okay, I'll be more responsive." In the former statement, the "agreement" is only an acknowledgment—the speaker does not indicate a willingness to do something different; the latter statement, by its generality, avoids a specific plan of action and is likely to be just another new-year resolution.

Yet another crazy-making ploy, one that is especially pernicious because of the illusion it casts on a couple, is described by Lederer and Jackson in *The Mirages of Marriage* as a "pseudoresolution." In this maneuver, one person suggests to the other that cooperation can be expected. But somehow or other, the subject under discussion—the problem at hand—usually manages to change, and the implied promise to cooperate never gets fulfilled. By behaving inconsiderately while giving the *appearance* of being considerate and collaborative, that

partner creates an insidious expectation that can slowly drive
the expectant partner to distraction:

He: Money is really tight. I would like you to keep the
checkbook balanced and up-to-date so that we can monitor
our budget.

She: (maternally) But dear, we're saving a good deal of
money on fuel this winter.

He: (confused) We have to keep an eye on the checkbook.

She: Oh, darling, you know how concerned I get about you
when you start worrying. Now, what would you like for
dinner?

The man leaves the house, and all the way to the office he
feels a tightness in his stomach. A dull ache is beginning between his shoulder blades and moving toward the back of his
neck. He feels somehow unsettled and agitated, but he can't
seem to relate these feelings to his caring, sweet partner.

However oversimplified this incident may seem, it actually
illustrates an all-too-common pattern. By assuming the "one-
down" innocent position, one person ingratiates him or herself
to the other, who can only conclude that something must be
wrong with him or her alone. What characterizes these conversations is the absence of a completed transaction. There
has been no definite commitment either to agree or to disagree. No decision has been made. The experience is not unlike reaching into a fog.

Corrective Prescription

Having journeyed through the problem-solving process to
the point of reaching agreement, it is now time to refine and
finalize. An agreement that is properly prepared will enable a
couple to avoid the pitfalls described earlier and is likely to
prevent further disputes so that healing wounds are not sub-

ject to puncture and old conflicts are not fought on fresh battlefields.

The suggestions that follow, recommended by Drs. Jacobson and Margolin in *Marital Therapy*, as well as by other leading therapists, are designed to chart a clear course of behavior change for each partner; out of necessity these suggestions are somewhat mechanical and perhaps artificial. It is important to recognize, however, that the problems requiring formal resolution are often longstanding and resistant to change. If change is to be maintained, a good deal of structure is critical *at first*. As the changes become more natural and spontaneous, the structure can be modified accordingly.

1. Change agreements should be very specific, spelling out in clear, descriptive terms who is to do what and when. Some examples:
   A. *Poor:* Tom will be more attentive to Helen.
      Satisfactory: Each day when Tom and Helen arrive home, Tom will ask Helen at least three questions about her day. Tom will demonstrate his active listening by paraphrasing or summarizing Helen's accounting.
   B. *Poor:* Helen agrees to be more careful with money.
      Satisfactory: Helen agrees to stay within the grocery allowance, avoid use of credit cards for three months, and reconcile checkbook at end of each week.

As with defining a disagreement, the key words in this suggestion are "positive" (agree to action instead of nonaction) "specific," and "behavior."

2. Both spouses should state their understanding of the agreement to each other in an effort to confirm understanding. During this confirmation and clarification process, press for direction by asking questions such as "When do you want it to happen?" "How would you like it done?"

3. Change agreements should be recorded in writing. Although these agreements may be subject to future modification, they often form the basis for long-term change and are

best not left to memory. Further, by writing down agreements, commitment is increased and ambiguities in communication become more apparent.

While agreements are specific, they also should provide flexibility; whenever possible, each person should be offered a range of constructive choices, any of which addresses a relationship complaint. Thus, a partner is enabled to demonstrate a commitment to change even though he or she is not inclined to fulfill each behavior every week.

For example, returning to Helen and Tom, rather than simply asking about Helen's day, Tom could have a list of options. It is understood that Helen would like Tom to:

Ask about her day
Call her at home from the office
Plan an evening out alone during the week
Initiate sex
Accompany her to the ballet

It is expected that Tom will do as many of these things requested by Helen as is comfortably manageable, ideally at least two or three times weekly.

It is important for a couple to view their agreements as independent of each other. For instance, the agreements between a man and woman do not have to match each other with regard to the number of options offered, nor should noncompliance by one partner justify noncompliance by the other. If this is allowed to occur, one partner is, in essence, given negative control of the relationship. In contrast, as the more positively committed partner continues to abide by his or her agreements, a constructive atmosphere is created for discussion and the commitment to change is strengthened.

4. Change agreements are facilitated by cues reminding both partners of their commitment. Since many of the behaviors to be changed are not part of a person's usual routine or are actually incompatible with former conflictive behavior, reminders are often necessary. In this regard, posting a copy of the agreement itself may be helpful; a code word "CHN"

("Consider Helen's Needs") placed conspicuously is also useful; and perhaps the most eloquent reminder of all is an acknowledgment of appreciation by one's partner when change is demonstrated.

It is suggested that couples allow a two-week "Fair trial" before considering renegotiation of their agreement. From that point on, however, either person should feel free to discuss additional options and modifications. If applied with sincerity and skill, change agreements will most likely remove many serious obstacles to intimacy. Both partners, by demonstrating their investment in the relationship and providing one another with a direction for constructive, assertive action, create hope where despair and discouragement were prevalent.

HEADING OFF THE IMPASSE: INTENSIVE-CARE TIPS

If after completing the preceding principles—support, communication, and conflict resolution—major problems remain unchanged, intensive care is indicated. This may be a time characterized by the suspicion or fear that the relationship is bankrupt or irretrievably damaged as a result of chronic hostility. This may in fact be the case. There comes a time in some neglected relationships when the memory of joy is so distant and the possibility of its revival so improbable that parting appears more reasonable than interminable pain and loneliness. In other instances, as with an individual attempting to survive a life-threatening illness, vital signs may be weak but their very existence is a signal of hope. For those who are discouraged but not yet hopeless, some intensive-care tips follow.

1. Whenever relationship distress is severe, a couple should reduce the number and complexity of tasks confronting them

by notifying those around them, including their children, to temporarily make fewer demands. As much as possible, work-related projects and extra responsibilities (e.g., volunteer activities), which add to a hectic, pressured schedule, should be postponed for the time being. In a sense, an ailing relationship, like an ailing body, requires special attention and energy until it is strengthened.

2. Attempt to do less together and enjoy it more rather than the reverse.

3. Carefully consider the possible influence of external circumstances that may previously have been overlooked, such as failing health, career setbacks, and life transitions (for example, the last child going off to school and leaving a housewife suddenly alone, or a midlife crisis typified by a concern about aging without having realized one's dreams). Remember, a close relationship should address itself to these issues, and avoidance will only add to the confusion.

4. Ask yourself, your co-workers, and friends if your standards are unrealistic. You may be setting yourself up for disappointment by expecting perfect competence, generosity, and reliability from your partner.

5. Consider remaining in the relationship on a week-by-week basis. Long-range plans are too overwhelming when discouragement is running high. Think about a relationship-improvement goal for *this* week (or day). Building one slightly improved week or day upon another can eventually lead to a renewed relationship. By narrowing the focus to a manageable time span, the pressure either to make a lifelong commitment or to separate is reduced.

6. There are occasions when it might be judicious to call a time-out; postponing a discussion can actually be beneficial if used properly. If the issue has wandered into forbidden territory or if one partner simply cannot deal with the intensity, a rest period may bring on a new perspective. Thus, when your tolerance threshold has been reached but the issue hasn't been settled, consider rescheduling discussion of it. It is worth some

lost time to prevent an eruption in which both partners emerge as casualties.

7. One of the most common characteristics of a distressed relationship is an almost complete lack of humor. Every gesture, every movement, every word, is taken with deadly seriousness. Laughter can sometimes be a powerful antidote to chronic bitterness. Indeed, psychiatrist Allen Fay, in *Making Things Better by Making Them Worse*, documents numerous instances in which humor proves to be the best medicine. One couple, for example, has been fighting on an almost daily basis for many years about anything and everything. The pattern usually takes the form of one partner saying something to which the other has to respond one better.

She: You're just like your mother.
He: Better than being a dried-out drunk like your mother.

With humor, the same scene might go like this:

She: You're just like your mother.
He: (starts putting on a brassiere)

In another instance reported by Fay, a woman becomes highly upset because her husband declares their relationship to be dead each time he becomes frustrated. Apparently with humor in mind, it is suggested to the wife that the next time her husband pronounces the marriage dead, she should respond by calling an undertaker to make burial plans. Simply by taking this action she is able to maintain her composure and, at the same time, highlight the silliness of her partner's ultimatum.

Certainly, not every provocation need be met with levity, but a sprinkling of laughter here and there can do wonders.

8. Give some thought to approaching a stalemate from a fresh perspective. A head-on confrontation, regardless of how skillfully it is worded, may not always work. An example from history reported by Paul Watzlawick and his associates in *Change*: During one of the many nineteenth-century riots in Paris, the commander of an artillery unit received orders to

clear the city square and to fire on the assemblage if the people refused to disperse. Knowing that a warning to disassemble would only anger the crowd and lead to many deaths, the commander *reframed* the order, changed its meaning, so that it would be received peacefully. While his soldiers leveled their cannons at the square and silence fell on the crowd, the commander drew his sword and shouted for all to hear, "Mesdames, Messieurs. I have orders to fire at the *canaille* [disreputable persons, riffraff], but as I see a great number of honest, respectable citizens before me, I request that they leave so that they are not mistakenly harmed." The square was emptied almost immediately.

Similarly, an imaginative individual, in tune (albeit in conflict) with his partner, can reframe a chronic relationship quarrel. One couple, for instance, was fighting endlessly about the wife's overprotectiveness of their only son. The more her husband accused her of smothering their son, the more insecure she felt and the more restrictive she became. This pattern continued with great psychological cost to all involved until one day her husband approached her differently. "You know dear," he began, "you really are a superbly concerned and competent parent. And I'm sure, *for our son's sake*, for his sense of independence and self-confidence, you would be willing to make the ultimate *parental sacrifice* by allowing him more freedom." Put this way—"for our son's sake," "parental sacrifice"—the wife no longer felt her competence was being threatened; she was now motivated to do something for her son, a challenge she couldn't resist.

Do not expect the suggestions above to be easily or quickly implemented. The greatest trap is to expect too much change too rapidly and too consistently. Further, particularly during this critical period, if you restrict your emotional existence exclusively to your relationship, you will, in all probability, intensify your feelings of being cheated and prematurely give up the struggle. A wiser approach is to fortify yourself on the nourishment that friends and individual interests provide as you navigate these difficult times.

CHILDREN: CAUGHT IN THE CROSSFIRE

Parenting

Being a parent, as Sigmund Freud once remarked, is an impossible profession under even the best of circumstances; marital discord can intensify the difficulties to unbearable limits. When three generations of family members lived in the same house or nearby, it was easier to raise children. Grandmothers and aunts could counsel and help a mother who was distressed; a couple that needed time to themselves to work out their differences could ask another adult they trusted to take over for a while. Husband and wife could discuss their parenting problems with older and frequently wiser members of their family. And the children could find a loving adult with time to listen and to counsel—a sort of court of appeals. Today's parents share the responsibility for being all things to their children.

Childless couples can sometimes reconcile their relationship differences and disappointments by ignoring the discords, pretending they do not exist. They can seek compensating gratification elsewhere, perhaps in their work; it is simple for both of them to have jobs. However, when there is a child, this shift of emphasis is impossible, and the child becomes living evidence of the dissatisfaction in the marital relationship. Here is a young mother's experience:

". . . We had been arguing for months. I was sure he was fooling around. I constantly accused him, but he passed it off as a joke. When he did this, I pestered him about it even more, but he just ignored me or made more jokes. It nearly drove me nuts. I nagged him all the time. He finally began to get fed up with it and told me to fuck off; he even smacked me around a couple of times. But he didn't admit a thing. It was childish and crazy, but I couldn't help myself; and the more I bore down, the worse things got between us. All this wasn't doing Patrick anything but harm. He was nearly eight, and he sensed the strain. He started bed-wetting again and even stammering. His teacher said he was nervous in school. Maybe that woke me up—woke both of us up. Not only was our marriage troubled, but we were creating a toxic home life for our son."

Games Nobody Wins

Discord in a marriage doesn't necessarily hurt children. Indeed, conflict to some degree is a normal part of almost all close relationships. It is when husbands and wives resort to using their children as weapons in the adult conflict that they are likely to suffer. Some spouses not only blame each other explicitly for the difficulties in their relationship but also implicitly involve the children.

For example, the wife may sway one child to her side and the husband another to his; sometimes they bid for the same offspring, and he or she may end up feeling like God's special gift to the world. A father deeply in debt who finances a new car for his teenage son, saying, "I owe it to him," is probably involved in this ploy, as is the mother who wears her threadbare coat for yet another winter so that her daughter can buy that new dress she simply must have.

On the other hand, a child's life may be made extremely miserable because his parents are competing to find fault with him (the "fault" allegedly "inherited" from the other spouse). This strategy is a favorite way of getting at the partner who is more sensitive to the child's needs, which is one reason why it is dangerous in a distressed relationship for a child to be a favorite of one parent. This invites misuse of the child as a weapon. In extreme situations, it may even result in physical cruelties. In any case, the child is apt to suffer emotionally, either through overindulgence of his whims or severe deprivation. The outcome is likely to be the child's loss of respect for the parents and a perpetuation of infantile behavior. Moreover, the parents' conflicts, rather than diminishing, are likely to be increased.

Susan is a high-level executive for a women's-wear manufacturer. She travels a good deal, and her husband, Robert, resents her being more successful than he. As a strategy against her, Robert begins to pamper their only child, whom he wishes to alienate from Susan in order to distract her from her career ambitions.

He: (disgusted) You're not doing your job. Jeremy is being neglected.

She: (angry) You're crazy!

He: (self-righteously) What do you mean "crazy"? You're never around to take care of him. You're always running off.

She: (insistent) Jeremy gets excellent care. Since when did you become father of the year?

He: (accusing) How many nights have you been gone— doing who the hell knows what?—and the baby woke up and I had to take him into our bed!

She: (counterattacking) What the hell are you taking a five-year-old into our bed for? Jeremy is well aware of my job and shouldn't ordinarily have any difficulty with it. Are you forgetting the times he has come to work with me and gone on trips with me? What about that? What about the time I spent with him explaining how I always come back? What are you trying to create?

He: (angry) I don't like it, goddamn it!

She: (accusing) That's it! It's *you* who has the problem. You resent me having an independent life. Your male ego's threatened!

Eventually, Robert's destructive strategy succeeded to the point where Jeremy started recoiling from his mother when she returned home from her business trips. Susan and Robert were divorced a year later.

Another common form of child abuse occurs when children are used to undermine a mate's authority and power. A wife may do this by subtly or not so subtly encouraging or assisting the children to break the rules established by their father. For example, as the father backs down the driveway, he notices the children's toys in his path. He gets out of the car; throws the bicycles, baseball bats, trucks, and skates out of the way; dashes into the house; and shouts, "Goddamn it, Gail! Have the kids keep the driveway clear. They have plenty of room to play all over the place. The driveway is off limits!" That night, returning from work, he hears the crunch of toys under the car wheels as he pulls into the driveway. He is furious. Storming into the house, he finds the family at the dinner table. Repeating the morning scene, he screams, "Who the hell left the toys in the driveway! How many times . . ." Gail, looking relaxed and unhurried, replies coyly. "John, it's probably my fault. I was on the phone with Joan Edwards . . . you remember her, the one you found so attractive at the Smiths' party last week—and I completely forgot about talking to the children." The husband turns, slams the door behind him, and closes the first act of "I'll Get You."

A related ploy for expressing hostility to a mate is "Victim-Villain." In one typical case, Nancy returns from shopping late on a Saturday afternoon. Her children had been assigned to do the dishes in her absence. As she drives up to her home, she honks her horn, but nobody comes to help with the shopping bags. The kitchen is a mess, nothing's been touched, and dishes are everywhere. Furious, she races upstairs, shuts off the blaring television, and angrily confronts her two children, aged ten and twelve. She yells, "What is the meaning of all this? How could you be so inconsiderate?" At this moment, her husband, Henry, who was reading his newspaper in the backyard, appears and is requested by Nancy to intercede. In complying with his wife's request, Henry allows his children to see that he is condescending to their mother. He implies, "My heart really isn't in this, but I'd better say these things to get your mother off our backs." In admonishing the children, he manages to uphold his image as fellow victim and adds to his wife's image as villain. He is widening the gap between himself and his wife, and between his wife and the children—to the eventual disadvantage of all.

It might be emphasized that in both "I'll Get You" and "Victim-Villain," the issue is not parental disagreement about the children's behavior. Of course, important family decisions concerning children are best made jointly by mothers and fathers; an authentic united front makes excellent sense because it gives children clear-cut direction to follow or rebel against. On more trivial issues, parental agreement is not critical. Nevertheless, the behavior depicted above is the result of a hidden agenda, and to focus on parenting techniques would be to miss the point. The critical issue here is underlying hostility communicated to a mate through the children, to everyone's detriment. Jim and Martha's fight about their children that turns out not to be about their children at all may provide additional clarification:

She: You're too soft on the kids. You can't just let them do whatever they want.

He: I don't know what you are talking about. I simply told Bobby I'd rather he didn't go over to his friend's house. I didn't insist and he decided to go anyway. Is that a crime?

She: That's not the point. It's because you didn't insist that I have to take all the responsibility for the kids. Who disciplines them? Me!

He: I don't agree. I do my part. What the hell is bugging you?

She: (angrily) You're driving me crazy! I do all the dirty work. You prance through life without a care in the world. What is this? If you're not going to be home half the time, the least you can do is face up to your responsibilities when you're here.

He: (interrupting) You're angry because the kids and I

have such a good relationship. You're always trying to make me the "heavy."

She: Oh, bull!

He: Listen. I take enough responsibility trying to earn a living. I think I deal with the kids just fine.

She: How do you know how well you deal with them? You're away so much of the time, you hardly see them.

He: (uncomfortable, interrupting again) Come on, let's forget this, we're not getting anywhere.

Jim and Martha thought they were battling about parental authority, "doing a good job of raising the kids," and the role of the "man of the house," but these proved to be superficial issues camouflaging more intimate ones that neither dared confront. It emerged that Martha felt left out of Jim's life—unattended, unattractive, and jealous of the time he devoted to his work. When Jim and Martha sought marital therapy, Martha learned to level about her real feelings, wants, and expectations. The issue of disciplining the children was never raised again.

Yet another tactic for wreaking psychological havoc is employed by the parent who makes abusive remarks about the other parent in the presence of the children. This usually produces embarrassment and anger in the offended parent and is quite unsettling to the children. Often the accusation is delivered in the heat of battle: "Don't give me that 'control yourself' crap. Why don't you control your boss and try holding a job for a change!" The rationalization here is "It's better to be honest with the children." But, of course, this type of fraudulent honesty is likely to put the children in the center of a game of "Charge and Countercharge." Also under the guise of being "open with the children," one parent is covertly pleading, "poor little me."

Margaret, a fourteen-year-old, describes her experience with this parental maneuver:

"My parents seem to be always fighting. They fight over the

most ridiculous things. Sometimes, when they're both home, I go to a friend's house just to get some peace and quiet.

". . . Last Saturday my father suggested we take a ride to the beach. Just me and him. When we got there, we walked around a little, then we sat and talked. He told me my mother was a sloppy housekeeper, a selfish person, and a bad wife. He said he tries very hard to be a good husband and a good father but that my mother makes things hard. I was so embarrassed and uncomfortable, I didn't know what to say, so I just sat there frozen. I didn't say anything to my mother, but a couple of days later, she started to talk to me, and she said the same things about him! She said she tries to make us a decent home, but my father is immature and doesn't want the responsibility of a family. It was disgusting. I felt so alone."

The parental games described above and variations on the same themes allow marriage partners to show superiority, cover up guilt feelings, hurt a mate, achieve superficial closeness and avoid intimacy, feel justified in "giving up," and so on. These ends are shortsighted, and the tactics are self- and relationship-defeating because they conceal rather than clarify the real issues. Strong feelings of jealousy, guilt, insecurity, and resentment, if not discussed openly, drain a relationship.

Dr. George Bach, in his valuable book *The Intimate Enemy*, adds to and summarizes the roles children may play in the marital conflict:

Kids can be—and often are—used as:

1. *Targets*. This is most likely to happen when parents shift the brunt of their adult battles from spouse to child.
2. *Mediators*. The father says, "Tell Mommy to be nice to Daddy."
3. *Spies*. The mother says, "Go and find out what mood Daddy is in."
4. *Messengers*. The mother says, "Tell your daddy that

I'd like to come back to him, but make sure he thinks it's your own idea."

5. *District attorneys*. The mother says, "I can't stand your father. But I'll stick with him because of you." Whereupon a child may say, "I'll help you get rid of him."

6. *Translators*. The child says, "Daddy didn't mean that. What he meant was . . ."

7. *Monitors*. The child says, "Mummy didn't say that, what she said was . . ."

8. *Referees*. The child says, "Why don't you let Mummy explain a little more? Let her talk."

9. *Cupids*. Parents, especially fathers, often cast their children as love releasers. The way to a man's heart may be through his stomach; the way to a woman's heart is often through her child.

10. *Audiences at adult fights*.

Dr. Bach goes on to say that in times of marital discord, roles 1 through 5 are likely to be destructive, and others, particularly role 10, as we shall discuss later, may be either destructive or constructive.

Children's Games

Children also develop defensive games as a refuge from their own emotional distress. One such game is "That Will Teach You!" As in all manipulative strategies, the details of "That Will Teach You!" differ according to the methods of dealing with parents that children have found most effective, and effectiveness is usually a direct consequence of the weaknesses of a particular parent. For example, a boy who knows his mother is proud of a clean house will continually leave his room in a state of chaos. A girl aware of her mother's concern for what the neighbors think will carry on a loud, revealing argument in public. A son will flaunt long hair and bare feet before his conservative father.

A rather dramatic example has been described by Joanne and Lew Koch in their book *The Marriage Savers*. Psychiatrist Michael Soloman treated Ruth, a seven-year-old with symptoms of serious asthma. Dr. Soloman suspected that Ruth's asthma was related to family problems and decided to approach her condition by way of family therapy. Every time Dr. Soloman got close to some of the real problems in the family, the child would get sick and threaten to die. After he had worked with the family for nearly a year, focusing on the parents' relationship, Ruth said, "I think that I should be sick for the rest of my life." The mother said, "Why in the world would you say something like that?" This seven-year-old child answered, "I've figured out that when I'm sick, the two of you know what to do, and when I'm not, the two of you don't know what to do. If I'm sick, you don't fight. If I'm not sick, you fight." When Ruth's parents' relationship improved, so did her asthma. Dr. Soloman reports that Ruth had not been hospitalized or even seriously ill for three years following family therapy.

The "Divide-and-Conquer" routine is another favorite of children in distressed relationships. Seeking a gift, special privilege, a waived rule to provide reassurance, the child will play one partner against the other. "But Daddy [Mommy] said I could" is the opening line of this strategy. With a parent who is trying to enlist the child as an ally against his mate, this ploy is extremely effective. It works nearly every time. If the demand is too great and the parent refuses, a reminder that "Daddy said I could" or "I don't like you anymore; I'll go ask him, he's nicer" is usually enough to reverse the unfavorable decision.

"Buffering," yet another distractor, is initiated by the child and reinforced by the marital partners. It is not unusual for a child to drift into the role of mediator during arguments. Most often, he becomes a buffer because he cannot tolerate the conflict ("If they split, where does that leave me?"); and because his parents, perhaps sharing a similar fear of their own, become dependent on the child mediator to maintain an illusion of tranquility between them. The following conversation involving a child and his parents illustrates the process:

Husband: Damn it, Jane, I get so angry when you spend enormous sums of money on such ridiculous crap.

Wife: That's just like you. When I spend money, it's ridiculous. When you buy something, it's a necessity. You see things in such a one-sided way.

Child: I got into a fight in school today, and I had to sit in the principal's office.

Wife: Michael, you shouldn't be fighting. Someone could get hurt.

Husband: If there's a problem in school, you tell the teacher. Don't use your hands on anybody. The teacher will help you talk it out. Okay?

Masquerading as a "naughty child," this youngster produces well-timed interventions to set himself up as a target and to divert his mother and father from further argument. He has learned that if he can turn their attention toward him, they will automatically issue a truce with each other. Parents who are fearful of their deteriorating relationship, who prefer appearance to real intimacy, are likely to be willing collaborators and reinforcers of the child's efforts. However, temporary armistices achieved this way are likely to have a damaging effect on the youngster. Once he is accepted in the role of peacemaker, he may feel at fault every time there is an emotional eruption he has failed to prevent. Continued distress between parents will result in escalated anxiety and disappointment in the child.

Instead of being supported and nurtured by his parents, the "child peacemaker" has prematurely assumed an adult role. In effect, the child relinquishes his childhood to keep the peace. The effort is futile.

When children consistently play destructive emotional games, it is often because their basic trust in their parents' ability to love and care for them has been undermined, and they believe they can get the love and care they want only through manipulation. Such children opt for attention even if it is negative. This yearning for attention that finds its expression in "impossible" behavior will diminish when parents provide a firmer foundation of love and security for the children.

Other Considerations

Behind many children's games is the unspoken plea "I want you to know how I feel so that you will stop doing things that are making me so anxious and afraid. Show me that I am all right and that you love me." It is not always easy for parents to view matters in this light. It is much easier for them to accept obnoxious behavior as revenge for punishments, felt injustices, or other unrelated developments. Usually these proclamations ("Jimmy's always been a nervous kid; it has nothing to do with us") are an avoidance of more heated issues. Sometimes, however, a child's emotional reactions are not directly related to or are out of proportion with marital conflicts. With or without parental dissension, the process of growing up is stormy. Peer relations, school pressures, achievement aspirations, dating problems, all take a toll on children; and parents often become the toll collectors because they're convenient.

Some children, as well as some adults, have inborn tendencies to emotional distress and acting-out behaviors. This does not mean they are born with specific emotional and behavioral disturbances such as anxiety or violence, but they do seem to inherit tendencies toward irritability, introversion, or low-frustration tolerance. Recent studies at the National Institutes of Health show, for example, that from birth onward, children exhibit clear-cut temperamental differences. Long-term studies have demonstrated that the child who is inhibited at birth and in childhood continues to act in a similar fashion into adulthood, while the energetic, assertive child is more likely to become an energetic and assertive adult. Thus, an inhibited youngster who is naturally very sensitive may feel that his mildly angry parents are very angry at each other; because of his overreaction, he may anxiously anticipate signs of another argument breaking out and again interpret the next mild conflict as a great hostile outburst, thereby creating more anxiety, feelings of insecurity, and so on.

This is not to dilute parental responsibility. The quality of the marital relationship and the manner in which conflicts are resolved certainly have an impact on children; however, they are not the only considerations. Children have their own problems, and their distress is not necessarily an indication that the marital relationship is faltering. Rather, their distress is both a signal to examine the situation carefully for the contributing factors and an opportunity for parents to work as a team in providing for their youngsters.

To Fight or Not to Fight

Children frequently become upset by parental anger and fighting, often feeling themselves to be the cause of the conflict. This is particularly true of the chronically angry family. Given these realities, would it be best to spare the children this emotional burden by not allowing them to witness or be involved in marital discord? Many parents respond affirmatively, and with some justification. First, there are times when the issues being discussed or argued are too sensitive and therefore inappropriate for young witnesses. Second, and more important, parents who tear each other apart in front of their children in scenes reminiscent of *Who's Afraid of Virginia Woolf?* are creating a very poor marital model for their offspring. These are tactics to be aware of and guarded against. The continuance of destructive interaction is an indication that professional intervention is warranted. Indeed, the recent trend to treat the entire family seeks as a primary goal the modification of these debilitating family battles. Without intervention, far too many children are likely to grow up thinking that marriage is an excessively troublesome and painful arrangement.

Considering the disadvantages, parents can decide not to argue in front of the children. The fact is, however, that simply not arguing in front of the children is a poor solution. Not only is it a virtual impossibility to have fights that the children won't become aware of, but a lack of open discussion actually robs the children of potential benefit. The one critical guideline is to keep the fighting aboveboard. Parental fighting in which both partners stay with the issues and do not resort to crude, manipulative strategies actually helps prepare children for their own future marital fights and for survival in a very difficult world.

Marsha is a slim thirty-one-year-old woman with long black hair and dark, searching eyes. She recently graduated from the City College of New York and works part-time as a laboratory technologist. Marsha has been married for six years; she and her husband, Richard, who also works on a part-time basis, share the rearing of their two children. Marsha describes her parents' marriage:

". . . They fought a lot of the time. You could hear them four blocks away, but I think they were basically happy. I remember many of their fights being followed by a resolution, a making up. They said things to each other in anger that they apologized for. They always made sure I was aware of the apologies. When they got mad at me, I was told, "Being angry doesn't mean I don't love you." When they were mad at each other, I was reminded of the same thing: 'We may disagree about some things and feel very angry, but that doesn't mean we hate each other.' They taught me that a person may not like something about you but still like *you*. This is a lesson that's made a critical difference in my life. Rejection, for instance, isn't as traumatic to me as it is to many people. I know, on an emotional level, that I can't be liked by everyone. Rejection doesn't make me feel worthless. I also think I am prob-

ably more assertive than most women. Being wrong or possibly incurring somebody's wrath doesn't frighten me. I've
seen wrath, and it's not so terrible."

Richard comments:

"I like Martha's folks very much, and I agree with her
view of their impact on her. I think she was very fortunate to
grow up in a household where people didn't believe in facades.
Her parents don't censor themselves and display only their
best side. They are very real. My parents, on the other hand,
were petty, bickering, and indirectly hostile to each other. The
display of emotion was taboo. I picked up a lot of bad habits.
First of all, I didn't speak up when something bothered me. I
would sit and stew. When I did say something, it was aimed
at provoking guilt in the other person; I tried to get my way by
using emotional blackmail. The disparity between Marsha's
style and mine made for quite a conflict. It's been only in the
last year or so that I have learned, mostly through Marsha's
example, to speak up and say what I want and what's bothering me. No camouflaging. No beating around the bush."

It may come down to this: To the extent that unexpressive
or passive parents wean themselves from the notion that peace
and quiet must reign, they will have moved to a starting position for conflict resolution. This is possible without causing
undue harm to their children. In contrast, those partners who
are chronically angry are probably obsessed with the wrong
issues and would best consider their posture in light of its
potential damage to their children. Most important, fair
fighting—that is, fighting in which both partners are honestly
striving to resolve a conflict rather than to destroy an opponent—can comfortably take place in front of the children.
Ideally, children will learn by example to fight for their wants
and express their feelings constructively.

Naturally, some issues (such as delicate sexual matters)
should be aired privately. Dirty, underhanded fighting is best
done secretly. If this is the highest level of fighting a couple
can attain, they should consider professional assistance. A

couple can tell if they fight poorly by the results: one or both partners are constantly hurt, and conflicts are hardly ever resolved. Issues involving the children that are fought and refought but resist resolution despite compromise should be reconsidered. What if the children were not the issue; would another issue surface? If so, discuss it and see where it leads. Even under the best of circumstances, manipulative emotional games will be played—but as side events, not center-stage attractions. As parents become more aware of and are able to express their own feelings and their children's real needs, games of manipulation will yield to healthy and open communication.

STAYING TOGETHER OR PARTING: MAKING THE DECISION

When is a relationship not working? When should one seek a divorce? An easily applied guideline to answer these questions does not exist because intimacy is much too complex a process to fit specific formulas. Some general observations, however, may apply. A relationship is not working when you feel that you can function better without your partner than with him. It is not working when you would rather be alone or with somebody else than with her—not just sometimes but usually. It is not working when you think your children would profit from the absence of your spouse. A relationship is not working when there is no fun in it.

When, then, should a couple wisely consider divorce? In most cases, a couple should not consider divorce without professional consultation. When it is clear that husband and wife are not functioning together without severe physical or emotional damage to one or both, and that the destructiveness is irreversible or reversible only with an effort that is not forthcoming from both partners, a couple should consider parting.

Once it is determined that an alliance is not working and is unsalvageable, divorce is the best way to ensure the sanity of the partners and, especially, of the children. Youngsters are infinitely better off with divorced parents than in a subtly crazy-making family. Unfortunately, many couples caught in an irreversible and mutually destructive relationship do not end it. They persist, despite the lack of emotional closeness and the consequent psychosomatic illnesses, infidelities, disturbances in their children, and general misery. Here are some of the reasons for the deadlock:

1. The one who would like to initiate the divorce feels that doing so would be an admission that he or she is wrong and that the other is right after all. Or if one decides to leave, the "deserted" partner may try to prevent the separation in order to avoid the suggestion that he, having been abandoned, is inferior and the spouse who left is superior. These couples remain together not out of love but out of hate. As one woman put it, "I'd leave the philandering bastard in a flash, but I'll be damned if I am going to give him the opportunity to come out of this thing a wounded hero!"

2. Each partner may want the other to assume the responsibility and guilt for the breakup. For example, neither may want to play "bad guy" or "home wrecker" in front of the children, so they stick together in order not to let the other have this advantage. Little thought is given to what such an arrangement does to the children.

3. One or both may be excessively afraid of loneliness. Most people abhor loneliness, some are terrorized to the point where being left alone makes them feel like an abandoned orphan. They marry to avoid being alone or to be "rescued" from their parents; and once coupled, they cannot tolerate being alone for more than a few hours. This is like having a fear of the dark, except that it operates around the clock. Both usually end up lonelier than they were before they were

joined, and to the loneliness is added bitterness. For each is fragile and requires constant reassurance from the other. If this is denied, the "rejected" spouse withdraws and the other now feels rejected. The distance between the two quickly increases. Usually, these people find it difficult to be intimate with anyone, although out of need for reassurance, they act passionately and may have had a number of affairs. They continue together, quietly destroying each other, because of a fear of being apart and alone. They do not want to face what faces them.

Aside from the psychological reasons for avoiding a divorce, there are practical factors that couples offer for continuing the relationship. Primary among these is financial circumstances. For middle-income families, the expense of two households (not to mention legal fees) presents a formidable barrier to divorce. The financial hardship and the psychological needs discussed above should be weighed against a living arrangement that slowly eats away at integrity and well-being.

PART VI

PART VI

Seeking Professional Help

Better and Worse

Barbara and Mark are married twelve years and have two sons. Over the last year, Barbara has been involved with another man. She doesn't know whether to leave her husband or end the affair and try to work on improving her marriage. She suggests that she and Mark both seek marital therapy. Mark is bitter and complains that therapy will be a waste of money: "I'm not crazy. You'd better straighten yourself out or leave. I'm staying in this house; I'm not leaving my children just because you've had a change of heart." Barbara isn't about to give up her home and children. She continues her plea for counseling until Mark reluctantly agrees to give it a try. Barbara and Mark offer a summary account of their experience; Mark comments first:

"At the time Barbara suggested therapy, I was enraged. I'm a decent guy. I try to do the right thing. This is what I get in return? I thought, 'Goddamn it, I don't deserve this!' Besides being angry as hell, I was embarrassed. Going to a stranger and telling him that when I roll over toward my wife in bed I feel her tense up isn't my ideal way of spending an evening! On top of all this, I felt I was living out a prophecy. My father died when I was very young, and my mother remarried and divorced twice. I've always had the nagging suspicion that growing up in a broken home I was destined to end up in the same circumstance. This angered me also. I felt I never stood a chance. I was also angered about the possibility of losing my children. As a child, I knew what it was to lose a parent. I didn't want what happened to me to be repeated with my children. All in all, I was like a bomb ready to explode. For the first time in my life, the thought of suicide occurred to me.

"During that first session, I was beside myself. I had this feeling of inevitability. I felt Barbara was going to leave and that nothing would stop her. I felt the way people must feel when they're about to be executed. I felt helpless and empty. I remember that when the therapist mentioned that he understood I was in pain, I practically jumped on him. 'Psychologist or not,' I yelled, 'you can't know what I'm going through unless it happened to you!' He wasn't defensive about that. He said, 'You're right. I can't experience your pain, but I sense it; I also hear it and I want you to know that.' He said that in a way that told me he really meant it. I believed him, and it relieved me because I didn't feel I had to work at convincing him how bad I felt. I began to cry."

BARBARA:

"My choice was either to leave or to find a way of satisfying myself within the marriage. I knew I was driving Mark up the wall. He was starting to drink too much and he wasn't sleeping well at all. He was doing everything to contain himself. I married when I was eighteen—straight out of high school. My father was very strict, and I saw Mark as an escape. Probably lots of people have done the same. Now I was going through a re-evaluation. I really didn't see why I wasn't happy in my marriage. Why couldn't I get as much from Mark as I got from this other guy? I knew the only way I was going to work this out was with a therapist.

"One of the early comments the therapist made to us was,

'I'm not in the marriage-saving business. I don't regard marriage as sacred. I regard personal happiness as primary. If the two of you can learn to contribute to each other's happiness, that's terrific. If you detract and you are either unwilling or unable to correct this, then it's up to you to decide where to go from there.' I felt a little taken aback by his statement. He seemed to be implying we would have to make a lot of our own decisions about things. I guess I was expecting him to tell us what to do. I had secretly hoped he would give me 'permission' to leave. I remember asking him what he thought about me leaving. He wouldn't say, 'Yes, go,' or 'No, stay.' Instead, he helped me look at the consequences of staying and leaving. It was still up to me. I knew that in the final analysis, I would have to decide, but I was aching for someone to take me off the hook."

MARK:

"During the first few sessions, I had to deal with my anger. Barbara is even-tempered. I am angered easily. This was the case even before our difficulties. In therapy, I was encouraged to be more expressive and this felt good. I began to say a lot of things to Barbara that I hadn't said before. But things between us got worse. I said to the therapist, 'You suggested I communicate more, really express what I'm feeling, and when I do express what I'm feeling, what do I get back? Shit!' I was getting just what I got as a child. When I opened my mouth, I got a slap. The therapist encouraged me—us—not to give up. He reminded us that pain is not a signal to run."

BARBARA:

"After five months of therapy, we began to see some real changes in our relationship. The biggest thing that happened was we began to appreciate each other as individuals—adult individuals. We had been so busy catering to our view of each other's weaknesses, so preoccupied with taking care of the other person, that we were both suffocating. It was a tremendous relief not to have to take care of the other but to trust in his ability to stand on his own. This was liberating for both of us.

In therapy, we began to appreciate—if not always like—each other's honest thoughts and feelings. We didn't feel we had to be overly careful about hurting each other or causing the other to fall apart. We began to believe in each other's strength."

MARK:

"Finally, after several more months, we made a joint decision to terminate therapy. We wanted to do things on our own. It's not that all our problems went away. There wasn't anything magical like that. We just began to feel more like struggling with them without any extra help. I guess we had come to a point where we felt we understood and appreciated each other. We felt we could live our lives and be fulfilled even without each other. Also, for the first time in years, we were genuinely cooperative and positive with each other. We learned to compromise to our mutual benefit. Our relationship took a mature turn. We became more desirous of each other and truly enjoyed each other's company."

In this successful marital-therapy experience, Mark and Barbara are helped in several ways, some of which may not be evident from their brief description. They have learned how to develop clear communication so that the message sent is the message received, identify the behavioral patterns and attitudes that were deteriorating their relationship, take responsibility for their part of the marital disruption rather than blame the other, practice techniques designed to increase cooperative and positive behavioral patterns, develop the ability to negotiate and create workable compromises. These are the critical areas of intervention. To the extent that a breakdown occurs in one or more of these areas, relationship distress is likely to increase. A couple seeking assistance from a competent marital therapist can expect help in each of these areas.

Unfortunately, as another couple, Carl and Virginia, were to learn, therapy can also be a negative experience. Unless therapy is approached skillfully, the dissatisfaction and destructive patterns in the relationship may be increased rather than diminished.

"We had been having difficulty in our marriage for some years. We really didn't have a partnership. Virginia had the kids to mind, no job, few friends. I was busy all day in a demanding job, trying to rise through the ranks. I would come home after being gone for nine or ten hours and just drop in front of the tube. We lived in separate worlds. Virginia always felt that I was too dominant and that she had to subjugate her personality to mine. She was probably right . . . Then there was the sexual problem. We were married at eighteen, and in the beginning of our marriage I was very unsure of myself sexually. I lacked experience. I was uptight about performing. I had a very strict Catholic upbringing; my Catholic school-teachers and my parents seemed very down on sex: 'This is a thing you don't do.' I remember that the first time I mastur-bated, which was when I was about fifteen, I was chastised in confession. Psychologically, it was pretty effective. I felt guilty as hell for a year after that if I so much as thought about masturbating.

"Virginia is the one who called Jack for an appointment. He was recommended by a friend. We were both pretty taken aback by Jack's manner and appearance in that first session. He was a big man, with a very large bald head, and he was sitting in the middle of his living room office in a yogalike position. He was very informal and almost insisted we call him by his first name immediately. During that initial session, he encouraged us to accuse each other. I thought that one of the sanest things we had going was that we weren't into pointing to each other and complaining, 'You're to blame.' Jack said that wasn't how we really felt. 'What you really need,' he insisted, 'is to go through an emotional upheaval.' He made the point that I especially needed this because I was the one creating the problem.

"In our second session, Jack said he had been thinking about our prior discussion, and he had come up with the possible solution. 'I'm not going to tell you how to run your lives,' he stated, 'but I think you both need a broader sexual experience. Have this within your marriage,' he continued. 'Maintain your marriage and have coexisting outside relationships. This will test your commitment to each other. If you are really for each other, you can share this experience and it will strengthen the relationship.'

"My first reaction to Jack's statement was shock—and fear. He picked up on this and convinced me I needed this experience if I was ever going to relate satisfactorily to a woman. He said this experience would provide a definition of the real me. I would find myself. Virginia needed less convincing. She admitted that she had some curiosity about outside sexual experiences, which, I thought, was only natural, since her experiences with me were not satisfactory. So we listened to Jack and agreed that maybe he was right about the open-marriage thing. That ended our second session.

"It turned out that the guy who recommended Jack—my friend—was the guy Virginia slept with. She told me about it one night in intimate detail just as Jack had suggested: 'Share the experience.' I was devastated. I don't remember ever being so uncomfortable. God, it was a painful experience. Now I was ready for blaming! But who could I blame? I had agreed to this insanity. For the first time in my life, I became impotent. It was two months before, out of sheer desperation, I called Jack for another appointment. This time just for me—to discuss the impotence. He was very casual about it. He asked how long I had been impotent. I told him over two months. His reply was, 'Don't sweat it, you'll get over it. It's natural for these things to occur.' He started telling me about his own experience with impotence, but I interrupted him. His casual offhand just-lean-back-and-enjoy-the-trip manner was no consolation. I felt psychologically and sexually powerless. I left the office before the end of the session. That was the last I saw of him. I never heard from him again. The next day I moved out of the house and took a small apartment. The divorce came through three months later."

There are several points to be made regarding Carl and Virginia's brief "therapy" experience. It is important in a prior telephone call or initial session to obtain information regarding the therapist's credentials and point of view. Beware of the therapist who imposes personal biases (e.g., pushes open sexual involvement). This does not mean that therapists are not to have personal beliefs or that these are not to be expressed, only that they be honestly labeled as biases and not imposed. The therapist who views his role consistently as a judicial one in which he sifts the evidence presented and eventually makes pronouncements is, at best, inexperienced. This approach tends to be extremely damaging because the individuals seeking help are likely to devote their energy and ingenuity to digging up "evidence" against each other. The result is an escalation of bad feelings and an increased schism until the therapy and the relationship break down altogether. Therapists who side with one or the other partner on an overall basis rather than on a particular issue or as a temporary therapeutic maneuver are destructively reinforcing the false idea that at the heart of relationship problems is a victim or villian. This attitude sometimes emerges when, under the pressure of gender liberation, therapists lean over backward to side with the spouse of the opposite sex in order to "prove" fairness. The view that a couple should accuse each other and blame the marital disturbance on each other is decidely counterproductive. Bitter quarreling over pointless issues, particularly if it goes on session after session and is encouraged by the therapist, is not an indication of an "intense emotional upheaval" but of an incompetent therapist for allowing the destructive behavior to continue.

Danger Signals

How does a couple know if marital therapy is warranted? Relationship distress may range from overt anger to undisclosed dissatisfaction in the form of avoidance. The most obvious "red flags" indicating that a couple should consider the assistance of a professional third party are these:

1. *The feeling by one partner that he or she is giving more than the other, that the rewards of the relationship are not worth the costs.* In these circumstances, one partner may feel unable to meet the needs of the other, or a spouse may feel unappreciated or unwanted by the family. In either case, there are usually feelings of loneliness and isolation associated with the relationship.

2. *Frequent arguments without resolution in which one or both partners are left with hurt feelings or burning resentment.* Sometimes the conflict takes the form of consistent arguments over what appear to be insignificant issues. Constant arguments about the children are frequently a clue that the children are being used as a buffer between marital partners.

3. *Severe psychological problems or dramatic gestures— suicide attempts, physical violence, leaving home—that drain emotional energy that could ordinarily be directed to self-help.* Psychological problems can include alcoholism, compulsive gambling, frequent lying, chronic anxiety, and deep feelings of insecurity or inadequacy. Whenever severe problems are evident, it is important that a skilled therapist be consulted. Even if the disturbed individual will not agree to therapy, the other partner would be wise to consult with a therapist so that he or she can learn to handle both the situation and his or her own pain.

4. *Frequent avoidance of each other.* There are numerous ways people living together can avoid each other. Sometimes a couple manage to have other people around all the time— frequent house guests, friends for dinner, friends to share vacations, friends to spend weekends with—hardly ever giving themselves an opportunity to be alone. These are usually the couples whose divorce amazes their friends who thought they

were "wonderfully happy together." The television set is another convenient barrier. Overwork or overinvolvement in avocation pursuits can also be a danger signal.

5. *Overdependence on the part of one or both partners*. This can be expressed by constant "checking" on each other, not feeling comfortable and worthwhile without a mate's companionship, resentment of a partner's independent interests, living for a spouse's achievements, and being overly sensitive to each other's criticism.

6. *Sexual dissatisfaction*. This includes lack of attraction, affection, warmth, or mutual sexual pleasuring, and an inability to let go in bed.

These are some of the more common danger signals; there are an infinite number of variations. When should you seek help? Not after a short-lived, shallow dip in domestic dissatisfaction. A day's arguing over the children, a few days of melancholy or self-pity, a siege of jealousy: these are not necessarily signals of trouble. They are more probably the results of the normal strain of living in a difficult world. The key to the need for therapy is repetition, a *continued* feeling of resentment, boredom, lovelessness, hurt, and sexual dissatisfaction.

What Not to Expect

When we are children and we fall, bruising our knee, Mommy or Daddy kisses the injury and makes it all better. They do magic. When we get sick and the doctor comes, administers some pills, and cures our ailment, the doctor does magic. When we are grown-up and have relationship problems, we go to another type of doctor, the relationship doctor, expecting that he or she will make the relationship all better— like magic. Unfortunately, therapy doesn't work that way. There are no magic pills, no magic wands to wave. *A passive stance—"Therapy will make us all better"—is an unrealistic attitude that guarantees therapeutic failure*. This is probably the most common unrealistic expectation that couples bring to therapy, and it is probably similar to the erroneous attitude that the marital relationship will prosper by itself: "Now that we're married, the relationship will grow." Most of us are aware of the falsity of the latter notion, but it is a tempting trap. In actuality, a marriage works because the husband and wife work at it. This applies equally to therapy.

Other expectations that increase the likelihood of dissatisfaction with therapy are these:

1. *Marital therapy is a process designed to keep the marriage together*. This is *not* true. Therapy is designed to help couples clarify their own needs, wishes, and feelings, and to identify in their spouse those behaviors that meet their needs and those that do not. The attitude of a professional is likely to be: "My job is to help these people stay together more compatibly and productively or to help them separate as amiably as possible. Since this is not my marriage, it is not within my province to decide which of these two courses to take."

2. *"The marital therapist, being an intelligent individual, will see my side of things and straighten my spouse out. He (she) is really the problem."* Very often this is the hidden agenda. One mate seeks a collaborative relationship with the therapist in order to straighten the "sick one" out. If the therapist acquiesces, the therapy may seem to be going well for the "righteous mate," but the marriage is unlikely to improve. More likely it will deteriorate. A more productive attitude involves shared responsibility for dissatisfaction with the marital relationship.

3. *"I should feel comfortable throughout therapy."* It is not comfortable to change old habits; and because change is a primary goal, the therapeutic process is likely to be painful at times. Unruffled feelings are an unreasonable expectation considering that sensitive issues are being brought to awareness and confronted as never before. Also, the progress of the part-

ners is likely to be uneven so that when one opens up, the other may rebuff him or her. The result is hurt and angry feelings. A sensitive therapist will support the rebuffed partner, encouraging that partner not to give up while helping the other to be more responsive. But still it hurts. Discomfort in therapy is unavoidable; the absence of any discomfort is a sign that the process is merely superficial.

4. *"If we are sincere and work hard, things will improve immediately."* Change is neither easy nor immediate. A relationship may even worsen before it gets better. Dissatisfaction, hurt feelings, anger, and misunderstanding are not quickly cleared up. Yet there is a tendency, after a few sessions, to conclude that the issues have been resolved. Frequently, this is a premature decision based on a fear of uncovering additional problems.

5. *"We can always go into therapy in the future; things aren't that bad now."* One of the greatest exasperations of marital therapists is that couples hesitate to seek help until the situation is desperate. At that point, they come to the therapist expecting to be bailed out. By this time, the relationship may have been critically injured, and the willingness of husband and wife to work at it may be almost nonexistent. Little can be done to help such marriages. They generally break up in the end, and the partners unfairly ridicule the skills of the therapist, when, in fact, a Solomon couldn't have prevented the dissolution. If these same couples had begun therapy earlier, before things had become intolerable and all caring had stopped, they possibly could have been spared years of marital suffering and misery.

Types of Marital Therapists

There are three major classes of mental-health practitioners: psychiatrists, psychologists, and social workers. There are also professionally trained marriage counselors, who offer treatment services to the public. Since it is important to know something about these classes of marital therapists in order to make a more informed choice, a brief discussion of each follows.

PSYCHIATRISTS

All psychiatrists are physicians who have completed medical training and have obtained a medical degree (M.D.). In some states, a psychiatrist need not have completed specialized training beyond the medical degree to practice psychiatry; that is, a physician with no special training in human behavior can call himself a psychiatrist or marital therapist without approval from a public accrediting body. Rather than formal training in the psychology of marital problems or supervised experience in helping persons solve their most pressing problems through psychological means, the physician without advance training has been primarily schooled in handling patients administratively with drugs and hospitalization and in giving rudimentary psychological first aid.

Psychiatrists who have had advanced training, particularly those who have completed the requirements of the American Board of Psychiatry, usually spend approximately three years in psychiatric residence beyond the four years in medical school and a general (medical) internship. A good part of the residency may be at a large mental institution, such as a city or state hospital. In this setting, the people with whom the psychiatrist deals are likely to be severely disturbed, such as schizophrenics or chronic alcoholics. Part of the training period, usually about six months, is spent working with neurological problems (disorders caused by pathological abnormalities of the brain or nerves), and some time is frequently devoted to work in an outpatient clinic, where the physician sees a variety of patients with a variety of problems.

Some psychiatrists engaged in psychotherapy and marital therapy rely too heavily on medical methods, especially the administration of psychoactive drugs (e.g., tranquilizers). This is certainly not the rule, but it is most common among those psychiatrists with insufficient advanced training in individual and marital therapy. Lacking the proper experience to intervene effectively with individuals and couples seeking to resolve nonmedical problems of living, the insufficiently trained psychiatrist is likely to prescribe tranquilizers in an effort to help his anxious patient. Unfortunately, problems of living are rarely solved by tranquilizers. Drugs may temporarily ease anxiety; but if effective therapy is not pursued, self-defeating patterns are unlikely to be reversed.

Ascertaining the psychiatrist's methods of practice may be accomplished in several ways. Talking with patients who have seen him in therapy may be helpful. Also, the psychiatrist may briefly discuss his orientation in a telephone conversation. If nothing is known about the psychiatrist except that he is qualified—that he has an M.D. and has completed the requirements for the American Board of Psychiatry—an initial consultation is wise. The couple should arrange to meet the therapist together, and jointly inquire into his methods and point of view. Asking pointed questions of the therapist as to his training, experience, and attitudes may seem rude or unnecessary, but it should be remembered that therapy is an important and usually expensive venture whose whole success depends, in large part, upon the choice of the proper therapist. Couples may have to visit two or three different psychiatrists before they find an individual with whom they both feel comfortable and confident.

To learn whether a psychiatrist is actually board-certified, consult a volume called *The Directory of Medical Specialists* at a local library or medical school. Or write:

The American Board of Psychiatry and Neurology
1603 Orrington Avenue
Evanston, Illinois 60201

PSYCHOLOGISTS

A professional psychologist is an individual who has a doctoral degree from a regionally accredited university or professional school in a program that is primarily psychological in content. The doctoral degree takes four or five years beyond the four-year undergraduate degree to be completed. This includes a one-year supervised internship. All states have laws regulating the practices of psychologists. In the case of psychological practice that involves service for a fee (such as marital therapy), appropriate registration, certification, or licensing is required. Most states forbid anyone not so registered, certified, or licensed to represent to the public any title or description of services for a fee incorporating the words "psychology," "psychological," or "psychologist." In addition to state laws, to be listed in the National Register of Health Service Providers in Psychology (available in most public libraries), a psychologist must have two years of supervised experience in health services, of which at least one year is postdoctoral and one year is in an organized health-service training program. Because a psychologist does not have a medical degree (in psychology the doctorate is the Ph.D., Ed.D, or Psy.D.), he is not allowed to administer drugs or other forms of physical treatment, such as insulin or electric shock. If chemotherapy is deemed necessary, the psychologist must refer the patient to a medical doctor for this treatment.

All psychologists are concerned with the dynamics of personality and behavior, but their training varies considerably. Although as a group psychologists have far more extensive training in principles of human behavior than the general run of psychiatrists or social workers, they may not have specialized training in applying their knowledge to individual or marital disturbances. Some have a strong background in experimental psychology, which includes testing theories of behavior on lower animals. Others focus on industrial psychology or personnel management, fields that have little relevance to marriage counseling. Psychologists in the private or agency practice of individual and marital therapy usually have a background in the more therapy-relevant specialties of clinical or counseling psychology, but it is wise to ask the practitioner about his or her specific experience. The National Register of Health Service Providers in Psychology mentioned above lists the names of several thousand psychologists who have applied for and met the licensure and experience requirements for inclusion. Psychologists are listed alphabetically and geographically by city and state. If this valuable resource is not available in your local library, referral information may be obtained by writing:

The Council for the National Register of Health
   Service Providers in Psychology
1200 Seventeenth Street, N.W., Suite 403
Washington, D.C. 20036
Tel. (202) 833–7568

SOCIAL WORKERS

The minimum standard for a professional social worker is a master's degree in social work (M.S.W.), earned by the completion of a rigorous two-year program of graduate study in an accredited school of social work. In addition to receiving the required classroom instruction, candidates for the degree work two or three days a week in an agency that offers counseling services, such as a psychiatric clinic, a hospital, a probation department, a welfare department, or a family-counseling clinic. This internship, spread over two years, is supervised by an experienced social worker who holds the M.S.W. degree. Usually, individuals accepted into a graduate school of social work have an undergraduate degree (B.S. or B.A.) in one of the social or behavioral sciences.

Most states do not have laws that license or certify the practice of social work, but there is national certification by the Academy of Social Work, as well as strong local, state, and national (National Academy of Social Work) organizations that strive to enforce professional standards. Most social agencies are sensitive to professional standards; and in only a few, such as departments of county welfare, is the term "social

worker" applied to individuals who do not have the M.S.W.
degree. A couple desiring marital therapy would normally not
be applying for this service at a welfare agency but at a family-
counseling service, where the professional degree is required
for employment. In seeking a private practitioner, a couple
should inquire as to whether the individual has earned a master's degree in social work from an accredited institution.

It is important to ask the social worker questions regarding
his or her professional experience. One pertinent question may
be "Have you had supervised experience in marital therapy?"
Typically, social-work students are offered a general program
during their two years of training. This includes group work,
individual casework, and community organization. A few
social-work schools provide for specialization in one of these
areas. Thus, a student interested in training in marital and
family therapy may be assigned a family-counseling agency
for internship. Others may seek specialized training after ob-
taining the graduate degree. Although social workers are frequently given less status by the public and by other professionals, with appropriate training they are as qualified to do
marital therapy as psychiatrists and psychologists trained in
this area. It is not so much the professional title as the individual's training, experience, and personal qualities that determine a successful therapy relationship.

To check qualifications or find a nationally certified social
worker write:

National Association of Social Workers
1425 H. Street, N.W., Suite 600
Washington, D.C. 20005
Tel: (202) 628–6800

MARRIAGE COUNSELORS

"Marriage counselor" is a general term that can include
social workers, psychologists, psychiatrists, pastoral counselors, and individuals with a master's or doctorate degree in

psychology, family relations, educational psychology, guidance counseling, or religion. Many of these counselors have received neither theoretical instruction nor practical supervised experience related to marital problems. Some, however, such as those majoring in family relations or marriage counseling, have received excellent training. Perhaps an important factor in allowing those with inadequate clinical background to practice is that in most states the title "marriage counselor" is unregulated. Only a few states have specific regulations concerning marriage counseling. Although anyone can practice in this field in those states where there are no regulations, there is a national organization for accrediting and certifying practitioners:

> The American Association of Marriage & Family
> Therapists
> 225 Yale Avenue
> Claremont, California 91711
> Tel: (714) 621–4749

Membership in this organization of several thousand is strictly voluntary, but the qualifications for accreditation are rigorous. To become a member, a counselor must have a graduate degree in one of the behavioral sciences plus at least two years of clinical experience in marriage counseling under supervision approved by the association. A couple contacting the AAMFT will be supplied with a list of three or more accredited counselors in their geographic area.

The Search

There are several ways to select a therapist that are likely to result in a satisfactory experience. If your problem is not urgent, learn all you can about sources of help in your area. In some communities, leading therapists are fairly well known not only in their own neighborhoods and oraganizations, but to the public in general. Perhaps they give lectures, serve on public committees, or are involved in community affairs. Often, you can form at least an initial impression through this type of contact. Sometimes recommendations made by friends, physicians, and lawyers are useful. These people may be able to direct you immediately to the assistance you seek, or they may introduce you to someone who knows the mental-health system well, for example, a psychological professional or someone who works in a community health agency that frequently refers people for help.

If your first attempts at using friends, relatives, and other professionals to find proper help do not provide enough information, try more formal methods. The following sources may be checked:

1. A local consumer's guide to professional services
2. Information and referral services, such as a community service organization
3. An area mental-health association
4. Local clinics, hospitals, or universities
5. Local or central branches of professional organizations

Although these sources are likely to provide comprehensive information, they generally must maintain an impartial attitude and are therefore not likely to offer a candid evaluation of a particular practitioner or agency. Public reputation is often a clue, but sometimes the popular therapist is the one who pleases rather than effectively intervenes.

Some marital therapists without academic credentials are very talented. However, in a field where incompetence and fraud are not uncommon, it is safer to choose a therapist who has had reputable training and experience. Unfortunately, professional qualifications do not indicate whether a therapist has had minimal, uninspired, or top-quality preparation. Further, since all forms of therapy are a mixture of art and science, the personality of the therapist is also important. A marital therapist may be a happily married man or woman who accepts life, marriage, and people, or a dour individual whose marriage is sterile and who approaches marital problems with a what-can-you-expect attitude. Each therapist's concept of therapy is a result of his training, reading, thinking, study, and discussion, his experience as a therapist, the types of people he has worked with, the success he has had, the profession he represents, and most of all, the kind of person he is himself. Therapists authoritarian in nature tend to view therapy as a formal doctor-patient relationship in which the patient places him or herself in the doctor's hands for diagnosis and treatment. Other therapists adopt a decidedly humanistic stance and see therapy as a relationship between equals—although one is an expert in psychological therapy—designed to facilitate new growth rather than to repair diseased or damaged parts. Those with a more conservative orientation perceive it as a problem-solving process, while still others hold to more ambitious goals and view therapy as a means of teaching people to become better problem solvers themselves.

Sometimes marital therapists are very directive in their approach, to the point of becoming impatient or irritated if their clients fail to follow their suggestions immediately; sometimes they are so nondirective that their clients feel they are providing the therapist with an interesting hour of conversation and gaining nothing in return. Occasionally, a practitioner will have a moralistic attitude toward sex, divorce, or life itself that is conveyed in judgmental proclamations about "right and wrong." Or the therapist may have an irresponsible, "liberated," egotistical attitude that engenders confusion and uncertainty on the part of the client. Even the best therapist with the best training is bound to have bad days and is certain to do better with some couples than with others. And however well intentioned a therapist may be, his interventions cannot always be correct. The mark of a professional is not perfection; it is a willingness to admit mistakes and learn from them. It should be clear by now that a couple choosing a marital therapist must be cautious. Obviously, these warnings can be used to provide justification for those who wish to avoid therapy or who want to terminate it because the going is rough. This is not the spirit in which the cautions have been offered. Competent professional intervention has improved many ailing relationships; effective therapists have helped couples to reconsider their relationship and move in more constructive directions; this type of exploration is not being discouraged. The point is that for couples to increase their chances of reaping the very real benefits of therapy, they should be able to evaluate a therapist with some sophistication.

Whenever we go to a doctor, a lawyer, or any professional, the child in us is apt to emerge. We don't question; we don't trust our own judgment. In making a decision about a therapist, one's own judgment is critical. After credentials, personal qualities, and reputation have been considered, the final decision as to compatibility rests with the couple. The most effective way to make this important decision is to obtain referrals from several sources, including professional associations, friends, and other professionals, and to shop around. Admittedly, this procedure can be expensive and time-consuming, since a few visits to a therapist may be necessary before a reasonable judgment can be made; but it is also possible that the first therapist seen will prove to be quite suitable. To assist in making an informed choice, a list of fifteen questions to be answered after consulting a therapist follows. Responses are scored from 0 to 4; 0 = never; 1 = slightly or occasionally; 2 = sometimes or moderately; 3 = a great deal or most of the time; and 4 = markedly or all the time. Circle the number that best reflects your feelings and observations, and then tally the scores.

1. The therapist gives me a sense of being understood, of having an ally.

0 1 2 3 4

(Empathic understanding is important to practically all learning and relearning processes. It is the ingredient of the therapeutic relationship that encourages a person to feel less guarded; when a person feels understood, there is less need to deceive, more inclination to change. There is one caution in evaluating this characteristic: Understanding is not to be equated with agreement. Frequently, the therapist may understand but disagree.)

2. I have a clear idea of the goals I hope to achieve through the therapy process.

0   1   2   3   4

(The process of goal formulation may involve a redefinition of the problem. For example, a couple may begin therapy feeling the main problem is sexual incompatibility. However, it may become apparent that the sexual difficulties are the result of intense hostility between husband and wife. Understanding how they have become so angry with each other may be the initial goal. Often, more than one session is necessary to formulate a mutually agreed upon therapy goal.)

3. The therapist appears alert; he/she does not look bored or distracted.

0   1   2   3   4

(There are many occupations that can be performed adequately by people who are overworked, who are not sensitive to their physical and psychological well-being. Therapy is not among them. If your therapist is consistently tired or distracted, this should be questioned. If the issue is not resolved satisfactorily, look elsewhere for help.)

4. The therapist's suggestions for remedying my difficulties make sense to me.

0   1   2   3   4

(The therapy hour actually represents a very small proportion of an individual's waking time; therefore, in order to facilitate progress, most therapists suggest psychological homework assignments, things to work on during the week. If these suggestions fail to make sense over several sessions, something is wrong. Discuss your confusion, since clarification is crucial to continued progress.)

5. The therapist is flexible; he/she is open to new ideas rather than the exclusive pursuit of his/her own point of view.

0   1   2   3   4

(There are many ways to approach a problem; a willingness to consider different methods at different times, according to the demands of the situation, is the mark of a professional. Conversely, rigid adherence to a single approach is a serious limitation.)

6. The therapist is open; he/she will reveal personal issues and feelings when these disclosures are likely to advance the therapy process.

0   1   2   3   4

(The stereotypical therapist—an unemotional, shadowy figure—does exist, but this type of therapist should be avoided. Effective therapy involves a lively interchange between people. This means that the therapist should be willing to answer questions directly, occasionally reveal personal issues spontaneously, and respond to inquiries about his/her personal life.)

7. The therapist encourages me to confront problems when I attempt to avoid them.

0   1   2   3   4

(A central task of the therapist is to keep the conversation focused on the important—and usually uncomfortable—issues that many of us tend to avoid. A therapist who does this effectively may at times seem inconsiderate or harsh. In contrast, if he/she does not do this, you are likely to be dissatisfied with the results of the therapy process.)

8. The therapist is willing to examine his/her own behavior if it is questioned.

0   1   2   3   4

(Frequently, conflicts arise between the therapist and various family members. A competent therapist will not avoid the dispute when it centers directly on him/her. The therapist should also be willing to change; this may include acknowledging being wrong, apologizing for being inconsiderate, and so on. The therapist who, under the guise of professionalism, implies that he/she is always right is to be avoided.)

9. The therapy hour is productive; irrelevant issues and small talk do not characterize the conversation.

0   1   2   3   4

(Change is forged in the fires of struggle; irrelevant, self-serving issues—"Do you have any tips on the stock market?"—do not promote this atmosphere. This does not mean that every minute of every session requires sweat and tears to ensure progress. Small talk, for example, may provide the bridge that transports the conversation into important problem areas.)

10. The therapist is interested in seeing the significant others in my life—family, relatives, friends—when it seems productive.

0   1   2   3   4

(Psychological functioning is influenced by the way an individual deals with intimate relations, the way they deal with him, and the way other family members involve him in their relations with each other. If your therapist does not want to meet and tune into your relationships with important people in your life, therapy may fail.)

11. The therapist listens and talks in proportions that make sense in the situation.

0   1   2   3   4

(A sensitive therapist will regulate the amount of talk in consideration of the needs of the participants. For example, couples—and their children—are often reluctant to engage one another, particularly initially. The therapist in this instance may be more active while gently encouraging family members to interact with each other. When full participation is under way, the therapist is likely to be much more judicious in his/her intervention.)

12. The therapist appears to have characteristics and qualities to which I aspire; he/she appears to practice what he/she preaches.

0   1   2   3   4

(We can liken the circumstances of individuals seeking marital and family therapy to that of individuals floundering in the water several hundred yards offshore. Perhaps the couple or family does not know how to swim or, knowing how, simply does not have enough strength to make it to shore. The therapist is on shore and has been trained in many life-saving techniques, all of which have been tested in the children's pool. He/she can row a boat; throw out a ring buoy; give artificial respiration. But can he/she swim? The best therapist is one who, under the same circumstances, could swim to shore.)

13. The therapist is open to and encourages differences of opinion rather than insisting "You are resisting" each time I disagree with him/her.

0   1   2   3   4

(Authorities are often considered—and come to think of themselves—as the "last word," beyond questioning. In effect, the authority is the all-knowing parent, the client the ignorant child. This is an untenable position, and the therapist who perpetuates this childlike posture is antitherapeutic.)

14. The therapist treats me as an equal; he/she does not promote the idea that I am defective or unworthy of respect.

0   1   2   3   4

(An indication that you are with a therapist who treats you as an equal is feeling comfortable with him/her. Further, the therapist without an air of superiority is usually casual and informal rather than stiff and formal.)

15. In general, my contacts with the therapist lead to my feeling more hopeful and to identifiable changes in my life.

0   1   2   3   4

(Many people hesitate to assess changes in themselves because they feel unqualified to judge their own behavior. However, research indicates that in the great majority of instances, an individual undergoing therapy is a good judge of his or her own progress. If after a reasonable period of time—several weeks—there is little or no movement toward a desired goal, discuss your concern in therapy.)

A perfect score (60 points) is most unlikely. A rating above the mid-40s is an indication of a sound choice; a rating between 30 and 40 is borderline; and a score below 30 is indicative of a poor choice. In marital therapy, it is important that the therapist chosen be rated favorably by both partners because a significant discrepancy in perception is likely to add to an already strain-burdened relationship. As noted previously, it sometimes takes several sessions before a reasonable judgment can be made. Other times, couple-therapist compatibility will be less ambiguous, and a much quicker decision will be rendered.

Cost and Length of Therapy

One of the most important considerations for many couples is the cost of therapy. Professional practitioners' fees vary by region and from one therapist to another. The majority of therapists charge between $30 and $70 per session for their services; a session may last from thirty to sixty minutes. Most private practitioners have a standard fee, but some will charge less if a person cannot afford the full fee. Community agencies and family institutes, both public and private, generally have lower fee schedules and may even have a sliding scale based on income. Do not regard size of fee as a reflection of therapeutic skill. There is no relationship. Some competent therapists have a relatively low fee schedule; others bordering on incompetent charge fees that are exorbitant. Whatever the fee, it is not unusual for the couple to feel resentful. Payment for an intangible service is hard to accept. Most payments result in something that can be driven, eaten, worn, or flaunted. Therapy provides none of these.

It is customary to be charged for missed appointments when the reason for missing the session is under your control and you fail to give twenty-four to forty-eight hours' notice. Group therapy (for individuals, couples, or entire families) is most often of ninety minutes' duration and is usually billed monthly (fees range from $15 to $40 per appointment) regardless of whether you attend all sessions. This policy is designed to encourage participants to attend all sessions. It is important to learn at the outset the therapist's policy regarding missed appointments, frequency of payment (per session, monthly, or some other arrangement), and length of sessions. In addition, find out about insurance coverage for therapy. Many health plans provide reimbursement for the services of a qualified psychological professional. None will offer payment for sessions with an unaccredited therapist.

Just as fee schedules and administrative policies of therapists vary, so do recommendations concerning the frequency with which a couple need to see the therapist and the length of time therapy takes. In many instances, it will be suggested that therapy occur once a week jointly. Sometimes it is also suggested that one or both partners be seen individually. A simple difficulty may be cleared up in a few sessions. A more serious relationship conflict may require a year or more of therapy. Increasingly, therapists are concentrating on the day-to-day functioning of the couple rather than making lengthy, detailed excursions into each individual's unconscious motivations and childhood events. Thus, the trend is more and more toward short-term therapy—removing the major obstacle to self-help so that a couple can progress on their own.

Some therapists find it useful to make a "time contract"

with a couple. In effect, they all agree upon a certain length of time or a certain number of sessions in which to reach a specific goal. The contract—or goal—may at any time be mutually renegotiated. Whether time-limited therapy is effective or not depends for the most part on how a couple react to it. Some husbands and wives are distressed and distracted by the pressure of an imposed deadline. Others are challenged by it and work more efficiently because there is an end in sight. A couple would be wise to discuss the issue: Do we respond positively to time pressure, or do we resent it? Would we feel more hopeful if we set time limits, or would we feel that we had failed if we did not reach our goal within the allotted time?

Regardless of the duration of therapy or whether a time schedule is established, it is doubtful that progress will proceed in a neat forward direction. Rather, periods of stagnation, or even backsliding, are to be expected. Freud termed these reverses "negative therapeutic reactions" and ascribed to them an unconscious sense of guilt that barred improvement. While there is good reason to believe that Freud's explanation is ill-suited to the dynamics of many people, periods of "two steps back" and stagnation are part of even the most successful therapy experiences.

PART VII

Maintaining Gains: The Semi-Annual Relationship Checkup

As anyone who has ever lost weight on a diet only to gain it back can attest, the critical element is maintaining the desired change. Sustaining relationship satisfaction is a similar if not more complex process. Both weight control and relationship improvement require fundamental rather than superficial change efforts. New patterns of behaving must become part of one's lifestyle; temporary measures simply do not provide the basis for resisting relapse. What's more, the continuation of couple growth is complicated by the instability of relationships. Relationships undergo constant change, which challenges a couple's ability to adapt. Just as adults go through life stages—the carefree twenties, the career-striving family-building thirties, the middle-age turmoil of the forties and fifties, the adjustment to retirement and mortality in later years—relationships also move through life cycles.

Partners in a long-term relationship can expect to begin their union spending most of their time engaging in pleasurable activities together without having to make very many sacrifices. This is a time when there are few financial decisions to make, minimal household responsibilities, no child-rearing demands, and an undisturbed sense of freedom. Spontaneity is high, as is the novelty of sexual and companionship activity. The euphoria of this honeymoon period is suddenly replaced by responsibility and decreased freedom with the arrival of a child. Roles will have to be renegotiated, and the desire for personal and career satisfactions often enters into conflict with requirements of baby care. The "oneness" and romance that were characteristic of the courtship period have changed, and relations with in-laws remain to be worked out.

While both partners spend the next several years striving to prove themselves as capable, successful individuals, the line is crossed between "youth" and "middle age." Now parents of adolescents, roles once again shift as the woman in many traditional relationships returns to work. This is a period when a couple is struggling with many disconcerting issues. Closing the gap created by their focus on the children is paramount; add to this further role adjustments, midlife crisis, the stress of receiving job promotions that demand more time and effort, possibly losing a job, changes in family finances, and moving, and the load at times seems unbearable.

When the children leave home, there is the "empty-nest" adjustment and then perhaps the most difficult transition of all: retirement. This requires a massive role shift by both partners. Occasionally, a couple who have stayed together to this stage despite important unresolved conflicts are forced to face their problems head on; no longer can they buffer their discontent with parenting or career concerns.

Even in this very brief and admittedly quite incomplete sketch, it is evident that relationships are constantly evolving. Each stage brings with it hurdles to overcome. Sociological studies have proven this to be true time and again. As Marcia Lasswell and Norman Lobsenz document in their book *No-Fault Marriage:*

• Parents of young children show a marked drop in the amount of time they spend conversing with each other and a similar decline in social activities.

• Couple interests and couple activities fall off as a man or woman rises to more responsible job levels.

• Arguments over money tend to increase as a family's income increases.

• Sexual infidelity is more likely to occur when a man or woman reaches the late-middle years.

• All indexes of "marital happiness" begin to drop when a couple have children and do not rise again until the last child leaves home.

None of these findings warrants publishing the funeral notice of long-term relationships. What is indicated, however, is the need for *continued* application of the foregoing principles, supplemented with semi-annual relationship checkups. Although sitting down and thoroughly reviewing your relationship may sound like a foreboding task, it is actually analogous to the kind of health-care checkup we automatically give our bodies and even our automobiles—except, in this case, each partner is both patient and doctor. Done responsibly, with a format that encourages an honest exchange of information rather than the placing of blame, a relationship checkup can help both men and women learn more about each other's needs and desires; in so doing, it provides a sound basis for making constructive changes.

The questions in the relationship checkup that follow are intended to assist a couple in identifying and appraising the assets and liabilities of their relationship. The checkup is not intended as a test and therefore has no scoring mechanism; it is simply a means of bringing out information that can then be used to make a relationship work better.

The first step is to put aside an afternoon or evening when you and your partner can share several hours of uninterrupted time. Make sure both of you have the opportunity to read through the questions before proceeding together. That way you will be equally informed about the process in which you will be participating.

Begin the checkup by taking turns reading each question aloud, one at a time, allowing one to five minutes per question to record your responses on paper. Do not yet read your answers aloud. When you have gone through the entire checkup, allow enough time to reread the questions and answers to yourselves to see if you have anything to add to your notes. Do not rush your partner or allow yourself to be rushed.

The next step is to go over the checkup together. Take turns being the first to answer a question. (Your answers should be kept brief, with no comment given by the other partner until the first has voiced his or her complete response.) When both partners have had their chance to answer a question fully, the information that each has supplied should be discussed, pinpointing specific areas of satisfaction and dissatisfaction in the relationship. The final step, after identifying a problem, is to attempt to work out solutions by using the principles that apply.

You may not be able to discuss every question and answer in one sitting. In fact, you may have time only to deal completely with two or three questions. If this happens, schedule another block of time within the next few days to continue the process, and make sure to keep this appointment. Follow this procedure until you have discussed all the questions and answers, and reinforced your relationship-strengthening abilities.

Relationship Checkup

1. Is rejoining your partner at the close of the day a pleasant event? If not, discuss the most important reason for regarding your partner's return home as unpleasant. Be specific; for example: "Very often I return home to screaming children and immediate pressure from my wife to step in and settle disputes" or "As soon as my husband walks in he gives me the third degree: 'Did you pick up the clothes? Make those calls? Walk the dog?' I feel as if I have to stand inspection every evening."

2. Which aspect of your life gives you more pleasure or stimulation: your relationship, your work, your children, your hobbies, or some other area?

3. Describe five aspects of your relationship that pleases you.

4. Is your sex life satisfactory to you? If you feel that it is not, what suggestions would you offer for improvement?

5. Name five instances in the past month when you have clearly expressed appreciation for your partner.

6. Name five things your partner has done for you in the past month for which you felt appreciation but may or may not have expressed it.

7. Recall three ways you have annoyed your partner—intentionally or unintentionally—in the last month. How could you have avoided doing the things that caused annoyance?

8. Recall three ways your partner has annoyed you during the past month. How could these acts have been prevented?

9. Recall a quarrel that took place in the recent past. Did it end with bottled-up rage or resentment? Did it involve denigration of either participant? Review the quarrel and discuss how it could have been handled more constructively so that it would have ended with an improved relationship instead of a bruised one.

10. Have there been occasions when you wanted to show affection to your partner and did not? What was the basis of the restraint? Give full details of the situation and your feelings.

11. Name five enjoyable activities you've done together and five you've done alone in the past month. Which did you enjoy more? Explain.

12. Would you prefer more time alone? More time alone with your mate? More time in company? Explain.

13. What positive factors do you feel are missing from your relationship? Who do you think is more responsible for these deficiencies, you or your partner? Or is it both of you? Give

reasons for this conclusion. In addition, discuss each of the factors you feel is missing. For example, if you feel trust is lacking and you are most responsible, discuss the difficulty in this area.

14. Briefly describe three things that you have requested your partner to do, correct, or improve, which he or she has neglected.

15. Briefly describe three things your partner has asked you to do, correct, or improve, which you have neglected because you could not or did not want to make the effort in that area.

16. Was there a period during your relationship when you would have been more accommodating to the requests described in question 15? If so, specify in detail the factors that account for your unwillingness to be more accommodating now.

17. For each of the unfulfilled requests described in question 14, discuss the factors that, from your view, account for your partner's unwillingness or inability to please you.

18. Name five ways in which you'd like to change. Would these changes please your partner? Why haven't you implemented them?

19. Name five ways in which you'd like your partner to change.

20. If you have children, do they help or hinder your relationship? How so?

21. If you do not have children, do you want them? Why or why not?

22. Do you know of a couple whose relationship appears more fulfilling than yours? If so, what factors do you think account for their alliance being superior?

23. What are your aspirations and expectations for your relationship in the future? Be specific; For example: "I would like household tasks to be shared equally" or "I would like my partner to become more affectionate." Name at least five

aspirations. Describe what you are doing to ensure that these hopes will be realized.

Hopefully, completing the checkup will remind a couple that a relationship is always undergoing revision; change must occur if each partner is to remain responsive to the other's needs. It is this responsiveness that prevents or at least limits major crises and promotes intimacy.

PART VIII

Epilogue: A Hopeful Note

Our journey through the principles of intimate relating began on a sad note: recall, only a minority of men and women, as reported in my book *Friendship,* considered their partner to be a friend. Yet most of us persevere in our struggle. More people are marrying and cohabiting now than ever before; even the perpetually escalating divorce rate does not act as a discouragement. Some of us may be disaffected with our partner, but we are still drawn to the concept of long-term commitment. In this regard, let's conclude with a more positive view of what this relationship can become.

Kenneth is a highly respected, award-winning photographer and the father of three children. He is a man who is occasionally exasperated by his wife but most often delighted and pleased by her company. "She is," he stated at the outset of our conversation, "my very best friend.

"I first met Nancy one summer weekend on the beach. It was an overcast day and the beach was nearly empty. I was just about to return home when I spotted this tall, good-looking redhead sitting alone. When I approached her she looked up matter-of-factly from her book—*Elements of Embryology,* of all things—and wasn't particularly friendly. But I was gently persistent. She told me, finally, that she was completing her doctorate in biology. I was pretty impressed; she really had exciting, ambitious goals. Finding a guy and getting married wasn't a top priority as it was with lots of women I encountered. What struck me about her was that she was so alive, so interesting. After we had relaxed a bit, we seemed to have so much to talk about. This wasn't just a beautiful woman; there was a real person under that pretty skin.

"We continued to see each other, and the following year Nancy graduated and accepted a very prestigious postdoctoral research position at Harvard. For the first couple of months I commuted to Boston and we spent our weekends together. After a while, though, we realized how much we missed each other's company during the week. I moved my stuff up to Boston—as a pretty well-established freelancer, moving was no problem—and we found a little place. I'd come home after a day's work, we'd go out for a quick dinner, and then we'd return home, where I'd help her study until late at night. It was a grind, but I really loved seeing her progress—she has such a fine mix of the scientific, philosophic, and artistic minds. I felt about her as I had never felt about anyone. I was proud to know her.

"We were married that fall, and over the next eight years, our three daughters—Jennifer, Katharine, and Alyson—were born. Nancy is still enormously involved in science. She has a university faculty position, she is active in professional organizations, and she is a frequent contributor to the professional literature. I, as usual, am passionately devoted to my work. Our life is busy, hectic, frequently bordering on the chaotic. I guess it's always been this way—even before the children. There have been periods when for days at a time, we'd meet each other only in bed. And nowadays, with the kids, especially if someone gets sick, the confusion at times is barely tolerable. I know Nancy is concerned about the impact of her frequent absence on the children; I often worry about my time with them also. But when I really stop to think about it, they're getting along beautifully. They are thriving psychologically.

"There are times when I think it would be much simpler, easier, more harmonious if Nancy didn't work, if she were more of a housewife. I think of my parents—my father worked and my mother catered to him. Life revolved around him. Honestly, sometimes when I'm dealing with the girls and I'm hungry and tired, I wish my wife were a bit more domestic. But then Nancy and I go out together, and I see other couples looking bored with each other, hardly ever making eye contact, not having anything to say to each other. That's when I reaffirm what we've developed. We're *still* courting each other—after sixteen years. We always find each other interesting, stimulating. When Nancy talks about her work, her excitement is infectious. I don't know if I would be as pleased if I wasn't pretty successful in my own field, but I am. She has great respect for my work, and that means a lot to me. All in all, even though life with us is never simple, and sometimes things can even be very rough, there is no one I'd rather spend an evening with than Nancy."

No doubt, the way of life described above is busy and complicated; it calls for the scheduling talents of a network executive, the flexibility of a labor-relations negotiator, and the energy of a politician campaigning for re-election. Yet, although it may not be every couple's solution, it does provide this man and woman the mutual growth necessary for love. And this is the task before each couple: to discover for themselves workable ways to keep their love alive. However the task is achieved, whatever methods are used, it is evident that love does not flourish automatically. Quite the contrary, it requires considerable thought, sensitivity, and skillful relating.

Bibliography

Bach, George R., and Wyden, Peter. *The Intimate Enemy: How to Fight Fair in Love and Marriage*. New York: William Morrow & Co., 1969.

Berne, Eric. *Games People Play*. New York: Grove Press, 1964.

Block, Joel D. *Friendship*. New York: Macmillan Publishing Co., Inc., 1980.

———. *To Marry Again*. New York: Grosset & Dunlap, 1979.

———. *The Other Man, The Other Woman*. New York: Grosset & Dunlap, 1978.

Ellis, Albert. *Reason and Emotion in Psychotherapy*. New York: Lyle Stuart, 1962.

Fast, Julius, and Fast, Barbara. *Talking Between the Lines*. New York: Viking Press, 1979.

Fay, Allen. *Making Things Better By Making Them Worse*. New York: Hawthorn Books, 1978.

Gergen, Kenneth J., Gergen, Mary M., and Barton, William H. "Deviance in the Dark." *Psychology Today* (October 1973): 129–30.

Gordon, Thomas. *Parent Effectiveness Training*. New York: Wyden Books, 1970.

Harlow, Harry F., and Harlow, M. "Learning to Love." *American Scientist* 54, no. 3 (1966): 190–201.

———. "The Nature of Love." *American Psychologist* 13 (1958): 673–85.

Hollender, M. H. "Women's Wish to be Held: Sexual and Nonsexual Aspects." *Medical Aspects of Human Sexuality* (October 1971): 12–26.

Hurwitz, Nathan. Interaction hypotheses in marriage counseling. *The Family Coordinator* 19 (1970): 64–75.

Jacobson, Neil S., and Margolin, Gayla. *Marital Therapy*. New York: Brunner/Mazel, 1979.

Kempler, Walter. *Principles of Gestalt Family Therapy*. Salt Lake City: Deseret Book Co., 1974.

Koch, Joanne, and Koch, Lew. *The Marriage Savers*. New York: Coward, McCann & Geoghegan, Inc., 1976.

Lasswell, Marcia, and Lobsenz, Norman M. *No-Fault Marriage*. New York: Doubleday & Co., Inc., 1976.

Lederer, William J. *Marital Choices*. New York: W. W. Norton and Co., Inc., 1981.

Lederer, William J., and Jackson, Don D. *The Mirages of Marriage*. New York: W. W. Norton and Co., Inc., 1968.

Montagu, Ashley. *Touching: The Human Significance of the Skin*. New York: Columbia University Press, 1971.

Stuart, Richard B. *Helping Couples Change: A Social Learning Approach to Marital Therapy*. New York: The Guilford Press, 1980.

Vaihinger, Hans. *The Philosophy of As-If*. Translated by C. K. Ogden. New York: Charles Scribner's Sons, 1924.

Watzlawick, Paul, Weakland, John, and Fisch, Richard. *Change*. New York: Norton, 1974.